Consciousness, Self-Consciousness, and the Science of Being Human

Consciousness, Self-Consciousness, and the Science of Being Human

Simeon Locke, M.D.

Westport, Connecticut
London

Library of Congress Cataloging-in-Publication Data

Locke, Simeon.
  Consciousness, self-consciousness, and the science of being human / Simeon Locke.
      p. ; cm.
  Includes bibliographical references and index.
  ISBN 978–0–313–35006–1 (alk. paper)
  1. Consciousness—Physiological aspects. 2. Self-consciousness (Awareness)
3. Brain—Physiology. I. Title.
  [DNLM: 1. Consciousness—physiology. 2. Brain—physiology. 3. Psychological
Theory. WL 705 L814c 2008]
  QP411.L63 2008
  612.8'233—dc22   2007036179

British Library Cataloguing in Publication Data is available.

Library of Congress Catalog Card Number: 2007036179
ISBN: 978–0–313–35006–1

First published in 2008

Praeger Publishers, 88 Post Road West, Westport, CT 06881
An imprint of Greenwood Publishing Group, Inc.
www.praeger.com

Printed in the United States of America

The paper used in this book complies with the
Permanent Paper Standard issued by the National
Information Standards Organization (Z39.48-1984).

10   9   8   7   6   5   4   3   2   1

"Consciousness is a subject about which there is little consensus, even as to what the problem is. Without a few initial prejudices one cannot get anywhere."

—Francis Crick

Contents

Preface

At its outset, any discussion of consciousness is confronted by three problems: (1) how to define the phenomenon, (2) how to measure it, and (3) how to explain it. Often the borders between these three problems are artificially blurred—perhaps indicating a lack of awareness of the problems, or at least of the distinction between them. The result is a loss of clarity, or even outright confusion. Perhaps the mischief-maker is item number two, for how the phenomenon—consciousness—is measured may occasionally be allowed to determine the definition and provide the explanation while at the same time gracing the confusion with the distinction as science: and not only science, but exact science. Exact is used here in the sense of ex-act, or *out of the act*, which refers to measuring. It is out of the act of measuring that the physical sciences—the exact sciences—have evolved. But the act of measuring—the operation of measuring—may not only alter what is being measured but even determine what is defined and how it is explained. The subject is defined and explained in terms of the measurement. Thus operational definitions, useful though they be, impose attitudes, strictures, and constraints upon both the measurer and the subject of measurement.

For item number one, three levels of definition—reflective of three states of consciousness—are needed. The first definition is of potential, ability, and readiness. It defines consciousness in the intransitive sense, indicating the potential to respond but not the occurrence of a response. It is analogous on the output side of the nervous system to sentience— the susceptibility to sensation but not the sensation experienced—on the input side. Registration of input (I avoid the word *sensation*, for this registration also includes other inputs such as afferent input and perceptive input), known as experience, is often called awareness and constitutes consciousness in the transitive sense—the second rung of the hierarchical ladder. Paradoxically, this awareness, often conflated with consciousness, is something of which the subject may be unaware. It may function in the absence of subjective recognition of its existence. Recognition of its existence is really an awareness of awareness and can be called conscious-awareness. It requires an experience and constitutes an awareness of awareness of the experience. It is termed self-consciousness, meaning consciousness of consciousness— or consciousness of itself.

Item number two—how to measure consciousness—comes in several forms and determines (or is determined by) the level of consciousness measured. The potential, or readiness, level—the lowest level—relies on physiological, electrographic measurement in the human or laboratory animal. Level two, awareness, can be measured electrographically, but can also be inferred from nonverbal behavior. Performance, action, and autonomic change (perhaps recorded by galvanic skin resistance) indicate awareness but do not require awareness of the awareness. However, there may be awareness of awareness of the performance or action though not of its cause. Reporting by the subject—verbal behavior—can only occur at the level of self-consciousness, for what is reported is awareness of the awareness. That is why the subjective experience as usually defined (what the subject can report verbally) is of limited (or, more accurately, specific) utility in the study of consciousness.

The third problem (how to explain what is measured) reflects not only the difficulties introduced by the measuring technique but is also reflective of the fact that many *explanations* are simply *descriptions* of an earlier stage of a process. Reductionism is not explanatory, though it may be a necessary part of an explanation as long as one bears in mind that the output of a system need not inhere within the components of the system. Reducing an explanation to componential behavior may blur the distinction between structure and function or between module and system. Perhaps this means that a true explanation of consciousness cannot be found in the physical sciences alone. If you believe, as I do, that consciousness is a product (better described as a function) of the nervous system, then the physical sciences are necessary to an understanding of the production of consciousness. They are not enough by themselves, however, to explain completely—or even to describe completely—the phenomenon; and so to the philosophers falls the paradoxical task of trying to understand a function of the nervous system—consciousness—by means of a function of the nervous system—the mind.

Acknowledgments

I have learned from many people: teachers, students, colleagues, patients, friends. Three warrant special mention.

Paul I. Yakovlev was born in Russia and trained in Paris. He viewed America, he said, with the eyes of a stranger. In those eyes there was always a twinkle. From him I learned that, if you have an idea no one else shares, you have either an insight or a delusion. Perhaps my ideas about consciousness are a delusion.

Derek Denny-Brown brought to the clinic a dynamic physiological viewpoint, to the laboratory a critical analytic mind, and to the world skepticism about reigning orthodoxy. Perhaps my long association with him accounts for my impatience with most of what I hear and much of what I read.

Jean Hendry broadened my knowledge of language, increased my awareness of the non-neurological contributions of culture to human behavior and introduced me to Levi Strauss and Structuralism. She has been a continuous source of enlightenment.

1

In the Beginning: Introduction

Efforts to understand consciousness, which are themselves perhaps the supreme manifestation of self-consciousness, continue. Books are written. Predictions are made. Physicists, psychologists, biologists, and philosophers participate. The brain is studied, but an understanding of consciousness eludes us.

Still, the quest continues. We are not looking in the wrong place, for surely consciousness is a function of the nervous system. But we may be looking for the wrong thing. Quest implies a search for something, and consciousness is not a something. It is a process or a distributed function of brain. William James knew that more than 100 years ago. In "Does Consciousness Exist?" (1904) he said, "I mean only to deny that the word stands for an entity, but to insist most emphatically that it does stand for a function."[1]

I start my car. The motor is running. I look for the running in the motor and cannot find it. I disconnect the spark plugs. The running stops. I am not justified in concluding the running resides in the spark plugs. But I am justified in concluding that running is a function of the entire engine.

The neurological function consciousness has a morphological base. The physiologic activity of this base is a process. The objective, behavioral manifestation of this process is consciousness. Like many other neurological functions, it is multilayered and hierarchically organized. It is not a unitary entity, but has several representations, the more refined of which have evolved from coarser components. This is a principle of neurological organization seen in other systems such as motor or sensory. The coarse or gross aspect of a function is usually represented at what are called lower levels of the nervous system. These lower levels are phylogenetically older, and are closer to the periphery or environment. From these low levels and coarse functions more delicate, refined, and restricted patterns of behavior emerge at higher levels, usually as the result of a process that may be called inhibition (behavioral, not cellular), fractionation, or individuation. Taking away part of the coarse function exposes the end product, just as chipping away the marble block exposes the statue.

At a simple level of analysis the nervous system can be viewed as an input-output device, or as a stimulus-response mechanism. Responses to stimuli at low levels do not require consciousness, either in the sense of a state or of awareness. The monosynaptic spinal reflex in which a muscle contracts in response to a brief stretch (the knee jerk for example) is retained in the clinically unconscious patient. Perhaps the term *reflex* should be restricted to situations in which cortical consciousness is not necessary. Restricting the definition of the term to the nonconscious state avoids confronting the problem of whether all stimulus-response behavior, including high-level function, is reflex. Some phenomena we consider reflex (for example, the corneal reflex that causes a blink when the cornea is stimulated with a wisp of cotton) may disappear in the unconscious state. On other occasions it may be retained. This suggests that consciousness (at least as measured by levels of its negative) is graded, not unitary.

Consciousness is not an isolated entity.

As neural systems ascend or descend, more neurons, and therefore more synapses (the junction between nerves) are added. Input to the highest levels must traverse many fibers, cross many synapses, and stimulate many cells, often proceeding from phylogenetically older levels to more recent acquisitions. In the progression of neural impulses across polysynaptic networks the behavioral consequences generated may result from a threshold phenomenon, which is a situation in which a sudden qualitative change in output occurs from an additive quantitative input.

Consciousness is not an isolated entity. At the cortical level it is an accompaniment (multiplexed, perhaps) and a manifestation parallel with perception. Perception, in the usually understood sense of the word, is not necessary for conscious awareness. Brainstem function and cognition (conceptualization) may consciously occur in the absence of perception (as the term is employed here).

Systems other than perceptual ones also participate in the genesis of consciousness. The modality-marked sensory and perceptual systems, by virtue of their modality markers, are distinct from one another. The parallel systems of consciousness are devoid of modality markers. Parts are interchangeable, and one part of the network can subsume the functions of another part of the network.

Whether or not these networks exist, how they function, and what they produce will be explored in the following chapters. A point of view will be offered that will not propose an answer to the question of what is consciousness, but it may contribute to ultimately achieving one.

2

This I Believe: Preview

Physicists and philosophers, psychologists and biologists—still, the quest continues. How to study consciousness? Where to start? What disciplines to employ? Clearly, any productive approach will have to cross disciplines, be both physical and philosophical, and carry the risk, when done by an individual, of a dilettante in the china shop.

To start from the "few initial prejudices," let's accept as given that there is a world, there are objects in the world, and there are subjects who experience the world and its objects. Interposed between subject and object are a number of stages of change. Let's take "subject" to mean nervous system, because it is the nervous system that is, or represents, the self (prejudice). Interposed between the nervous system and the environment are the physical properties of objects (atoms and molecules), the physical events that transmit information about the objects (molecules, waves), transducers that transform the physical events (rods and cones, hair cells, corpuscles), cells and fibers that carry impulses (neurons, axons, and spikes), aggregates of fibers and cells (nuclei and tracts), and the conjunction of these nuclei and tracts into systems.

Activity occurs at each level, and a hierarchy of activity is established so that lower levels (that is, temporally earlier in the input cascade) contribute to, and perhaps somehow generate, the higher levels. Consciousness appears at one of these higher levels. How and where that occurs is the puzzle.

For the most part, we will pay little attention to the early links in the chain. Objects, waves, transducers, and even nerves will be put aside. That consciousness is a product of physical events (prejudice) is accepted. That these physical events occur in the nervous system (prejudice) is agreed. That neuronal activity is required for consciousness (prejudice) is affirmed. But we will not find consciousness in the neuron any more than we found running in the spark plug. So we will not look there. Nor (another prejudice) will we look outside. Consciousness is an attribute of an organism, not of the external environment, though some think otherwise. "Neo-realism is said to be an account of consciousness as outside the brain and head . . . consciousness is in the environment, . . ." and "exist(s) wholly independently of being perceived or not. Consciousness does not depend on brains. A person's conscious experience at any time is part of the environment acting on the person and nothing else."[1] I understand environment here to mean the outside world, ignoring that the brain is not only part of the environment, but models the outside world. Or is that the point of contention?—again not distinguishing perception and conception from consciousness. But this consciousness in the outside world is independent of "being perceived or not." As with objects, waves, transducers, and nerves, we will put this aside.

Perhaps a definition will help. Let's define the state of consciousness axiomatically as "the state of an organism able to respond at a cerebral level to stimuli from the environment." This says nothing about awareness, perception, representation, intention, feeling, thought, or action. It says nothing about awareness to allow for "automatic" responses generated by procedural memory or for response to subliminal stimuli. It says nothing about action, for response is not necessary, but only the ability to respond. It doesn't even say anything about being asleep or awake. It simply says that if the organism *can* respond at a cerebral level, it is conscious. But keep in mind that the brain is part of the environment it models. Stimuli from the cerebrum can elicit a response from the cerebrum. Of course, this definition really does not define consciousness but merely describes the state

> *Let's define the state of consciousness axiomatically as "the state of an organism able to respond at a cerebral level to stimuli from the environment."*

of consciousness (intransitive), because consciousness is a state that results from a process. It also emphasizes that this state, an attribute of the organism, is distinct from usage that speaks of "consciousness of" (transitive), relating to a sensation or percept above a certain limen. The state is sensible, susceptible, and responsive above and below the limen. This attempt at a definition gives us something to work with. The issue of consciousness as a state is complicated by other definitions. Pacherie, for instance, writes, "the notion of a conscious state can be understood in at least two ways . . . a mental state is conscious if, in virtue of being in that state, the creature whose state it is is conscious of the object, property, or state of affairs the state represents or is about (first order consciousness) or . . . a state is conscious if the creature whose state it is is conscious of being in that state . . . (second order consciousness)."[2] I propose we confine the definition of the state to a disposition: the state of preparedness or readiness to respond. Pacherie's first order consciousness I view as awareness or "consciousness of," and her second order consciousness I understand as awareness of awareness or self-consciousness. Of course, if the distinction between mental and physical (neural) is considered unbridgeable, and consciousness is considered an attribute of the mental, then the search for a neural basis (or even correlate) of consciousness is futile. In what follows, I generally mean the state, as distinguished from awareness, when the term "consciousness" appears. Awareness is a different phenomenon that operates at the level of awareness or of unawareness, and awareness of the awareness is something still different. Awareness of which the organism is unaware could be termed fore-consciousness, and awareness of awareness should be termed self-consciousness.

A further prejudice is that the nervous system evolved; there is an evolutionary continuity between our nervous system and the nervous systems of other animals. Part of that continuity is reflected in levels of the human nervous system. Lower levels—that is, those closer to the periphery—are phylogenetically older. Part of that continuity is reflected in the maturation of an individual nervous system. The phylogenetically older components are developed earlier.

The nervous system is a true system, a complex unity composed of diverse parts that in their turn may be systems. Systems and systems biology deal with how "large numbers of interrelated components . . . comprise modules or networks whose functional properties emerge."[3] The nervous system is modular, has emergent properties, and serves a unified function. The parts work together to provide a unified whole. This is true for consciousness—which is often described as unified—but it is also true for other neurological functions (the visual system is perhaps the best example). Though they are made up of parts or components often represented in different areas—even levels—of the nervous system, we experience them as a whole. How this occurs is the so-called binding problem, well exemplified by the visual *system* in which more than thirty widely distributed areas function together as a unity. We have no difficulty accepting the fact of binding or unity in vision even though we do not know the mechanism of binding. But somehow we look on the unity of consciousness (or, at least, some philosophers do) as different. I would suggest (prejudice) that consciousness is no different. It is made up of parts cohering into a unity. We simply do not speak of a consciousness *system*. Can we find ways to display the parts of the consciousness system, as has been done with other systems?

One way is by the dissolution of function that occurs in pathological states. When high levels of neuraxes are affected, lower levels are revealed. The parts (which, perhaps, are systems themselves) that contribute to the unified whole may be exposed. And they, too, may be unified wholes, just not quite as much of a whole as at higher levels.

More prejudice: I believe in emergent properties. I don't understand the principle of how it works, but I know of many instances, and I can even understand some of them. In many situations emergent properties are the properties of a system. Emergent properties often cannot emerge without a collection of parts, and, if what emerges is a unity, the collection of parts must (by definition) be a system. So it comes as no surprise that I believe emergent properties are an attribute of the nervous system, or that I believe consciousness an emergent property. It does not reside anywhere; it is not an attribute of a nerve cell or a collection of cells. It is a process or function of a system—that is, an emergent process. It is a manifestation of the function of the system. The emergence of a property defines a threshold (not the other way around as is often implied); it is a bright line before which the property was not present (did not exist?) and after which it continues, often unchanged.

The system from which this process—consciousness—emerges is composed of interchangeable parts. Replacing one with another does not change the configuration (and, therefore, the output) of the assembly. Interchangeability implies identity—or at least a great similarity of parts. One analogy is an array of lightbulbs displaying a message in a public place. Think of Times Square and the moving headlines on the old Times Building. One bulb can replace another. The difference between figure and ground is determined by a dynamic factor (such as voltage, in the analogy), which can range from being off to being bright (a ramp), changing the prominence of the ground (the barely conscious background context) in relation to the figure (percept or focused attention). The illusion of movement can be created. When the components of the assembly are different, one from another, interchangeability is not possible without changing the output of the assembly. *ART* is not *TAR*, and neither of the two is *RAT*. The interchangeability of the modality-nonspecific modules, without changing the emergent property, is possible, because the modules *are* nonspecific. Generalized consciousness persists even if entire assemblies are destroyed, because other assemblies result in the same emergent process. The process, or at least its manifestations, are widely distributed. Once threshold is achieved and a sufficient number of modules are assembled to allow consciousness to emerge, consciousness is generalized, although in some pathologic states it may have focal emphasis. But, in most instances, destruction or isolation of a significant number of neural assemblies does not impair generalized consciousness (the state), because a threshold number of assemblies elsewhere allows the property to emerge. Think back to the era of psychosurgery, when even extensive isolation of frontal lobes caused no measurable alteration in the state of consciousness. Thus the relationship is, in Honderich's term, *many–one*. This is what makes it hard to demonstrate focal, lateralized loss of consciousness in pathologic states. The interchange of modality-specific modules, if sufficient, will change the percept or sensation, although a certain amount of substitution can be tolerated without the organism realizing the substitution, as in a "recovery" following a small stroke. Recovery is never complete, as can be demonstrated by the effect of drugs such as alcohol, anesthetics, or other central nervous system depressants, which bring out manifestations of the recovered deficit.

This interchangeability, I suppose, could be viewed as the basis for the philosophic concept of supervenience, wherein consciousness supervenes on brain function. For Searle this is a *causal supervenience*. "The brain processes are causally responsible for the supervenient feature. The brain processes do not, at the level of neuron firings, constitute consciousness; rather the neuron firings at the lower level cause the high level or systems feature of consciousness"—what I construe to be the emergent property of an assembly of modules.[4] Honderich describes the proposition of brain–mind *supervenience* in a way that underscores the interchangeability. "Consciousness cannot change without a neural change but relevant neural state can be replaced by another without a change in consciousness. That is, the neural–consciousness relation is many–one."[5] For Chalmers "Consciousness arises from a physical substrate in virtue of certain contingent laws of nature, which are not themselves implied by physical laws."[6] He goes on to note that there are psychophysical "*supervenience laws* telling us how experience arises from physical processes."[7]

Because consciousness relates to the environment—the world around us with its objects, but also the body with its innards—it makes sense to look for the emergence of consciousness somewhere along the course of the input system of this input-output device called the nervous system. The input systems at the lowest level are marked by modality, because input is by way of the senses. This modality is present neither in the object nor in the physical events that transmit. Modalities are not even present in the transducers or nerves; sensory nerves do not contain sensation. To illustrate: the optic nerve does not contain vision. The impulses transmitted by the optic nerves and any other sensory nerve are very much the same. Even the pattern of firing does not contain the modality. Modality is determined by location, by site of termination, and it first appears consciously at a cerebral (to include the thalamus) level. This locating of modalities does not solve any problem but merely restates it closer to, or deeper in, the central nervous system. The modality is not in the locus. The sensation is not even produced in the locus but is merely represented there. Why one locus should represent one modality and another locus another is a major part of the problem, further expanded by introducing the notion of representation. Whatever representation is, it is not a homunculus. It is not biologically isomorphic with the object represented. It relates somehow to the neural events that occur at the locus, but it is not the neural events themselves. To speak of it as mapping emphasizes the locus aspect of it but does nothing further, even if mapping is taken to mean mathematical isomorphism. Representation, too, may be an emergent property. Unlike consciousness or some other emergent properties that we experience, we do not experience representation directly. We may not understand consciousness, but (like obscenity) we know it when we see (or feel) it. Not so with representation, however, which we don't know even if we see it—probably because we never really *see* it. This lack of recognition does not diminish representation's value as a concept—a tool to be used in exploration—so it will appear again.

Nerves contain more information than just impulses. A radioisotope injected into the eye will show up in visual cortex after being passed along the chain. A nerve to a fast-twitch muscle that is transplanted to a slow-twitch muscle changes not only the twitch but also the histochemistry of the muscle. But, whatever the information conveyed by axoplasmic transport (in both directions, by the way), it is not a modality; it is not pain.

Modality-specific input may function earlier than the level of thalamus, but not by virtue of recognition of the modality. When it operates at a low—for instance, spinal—level, a modality-marked stimulus elicits a response independent of the modality because it is noxious, not because it is painful. What this really means is that modality is not represented as modality at a low level. The need for acquisition of higher levels in order for the modality to emerge suggests the need for more components in the assembly to allow *creation* (that is, emergence) of the modality. This is why the collateral branches of the ascending, modality-marked lemniscal systems (which ultimately terminate in thalamus) can go to the brain stem as unmarked input. The marking does not occur in the fiber or tract but in its site of termination. So when we talk of modality-marked or modality-unmarked pathways—specific and nonspecific systems, respectively— only metonymically do we mean that the pain fibers convey pain or that the optic nerve fibers convey vision. Fibers only convey impulses. Where they terminate determines what they become subjectively. That is why a nonvisual stimulus, such as a blow to the eye, may cause you to see stars.

What I am going to suggest is that the sensory (in its broad sense, which includes all modalities) input to the central nervous system divides shortly after arrival into two systems: one modality-marked, a second unmarked. They then go their separate anatomic ways, one to generate sensation and perception and the other to generate (but not be) consciousness. Having separated in the brain stem, they will coalesce again, perhaps rearranged, in the cerebrum, forming a tightly linked, though separable, pairing of conscious awareness and conscious perception (or conscious anything—so long as there is a thing). If we want to talk about conscious awareness (which is what we usually want to talk about), we should call it conscious awareness. If we call it consciousness, we seem to be equating awareness (of a specific modality) with consciousness (generated by modality nonspecific input).

A final prejudice: I don't believe in zombies. If, for example, we are talking about procedural or implicit memory—instructions for performance that are usually, but not always, learned and stored somewhere for automatic nonconscious use—let's call it procedural memory. It is a perfectly good term for a process we don't understand. But because we don't understand it there is no need to abuse it with the epithet *zombie*. The notion that zombies *lack experience* depends on the definition of experience and cannot apply to procedural memory that clearly reflects experience. Zombies are defined as lacking phenomenal memory by Humphrey, who ascribes to Chalmers the notion of a "subject whose lack of phenomenal memory entails nothing at all," and they are represented by Crick and Koch's *On Line System*.[8]

A question not customarily addressed, perhaps because it is so diffi-cult to answer, is whether there can be consciousness (transitive) with-out awareness. Conscious awareness is usually treated as an entity. The equation of the two components simplifies the matter if only because it restricts the process to a cerebral level. But conscious awareness (like conscious anything—conscious will, for example) is a bipartite affair, a situation duplicated in attention. One cannot pay attention without pay-ing attention to something. One cannot be consciously aware without being aware of something. In each case the something is specific and is transmitted by specific pathways and nuclei. The intentionality of the philosopher is a manifestation of the functions of the specific systems. The other half of the dyad—consciousness or attention—is devoid of object; it just is. Consciousness is a manifestation of certain functions of the nonspecific systems. Attempts to measure or define it most com-monly measure or define the *thing of* which one is aware rather than the process of consciousness itself. Since intentionality is *aboutness*, it requires a sensation, percept, or concept to support it. To separate con-sciousness from an awareness of the thing of which one is aware (a sen-sation or percept), we need to find situations in which only one member of the consciousness-awareness pair is present. Pathological processes may uncouple the two, but the separation also occurs normally. Using intentionality as the measurement of perception, Searle helps set this in relief. "An example of a conscious state that is not intentional is the sense of anxiety that one sometimes gets when one is not anxious about any-thing in particular but just has a feeling of anxiousness."[9] This free-floating anxiety, unattached to a percept or concept, demonstrates conscious-ness without awareness, without intentionality, without some *thing*. The point is underscored by Honderich, who writes: It "is very widely thought . . . [that] not all conscious events have the property of intentionality."[10] And if you accept the notion that the sleeper is not conscious (I do not, and neither do you if you accepted our definition) then the converse exists as well, for "intentional states that are not conscious . . . exist even when one is sound asleep."[11]

To answer the question (of whether consciousness can exist without awareness) in the affirmative raises further complications. If there is no awareness, how do we know consciousness exists? And if it exists before the evocation of awareness, at what level of unawareness in the nervous system does it appear? The isolated axon has memory, of a sort; but one could hardly claim awareness or consciousness. Synapses and systems respond to events and are altered in response, but they are usu-ally not considered conscious or aware. Response cannot be construed as awareness, although it indicates awareness in some sense of the term. But it may be awareness without awareness. Only at a sufficiently high level—which means a sufficient accumulation of functions—does consciousness emerge. How to define this level is the problem; for, wherever it is placed, the location is arbitrary and by general consent. Most would agree that the spinal cord, though it can respond, is not conscious; and most would not agree that consciousness, when it evolves, is located (insofar as a function can be located) in the brain stem. Yet the evidence is convincing that the brain stem ascending reticular activating system is necessary for both the conscious state and conscious awareness. This system (which also includes other regions, such as the basal forebrain nuclei, the locus coeruleus, and the suprachiasmatic nucleus of hypothalamus—regions not in the brain stem but which should be understood as included in the term ascending, reticular activating system) primes the cortex, permitting it to become aware of the cortical input, which otherwise might be received without awareness. "[M]idbrain reticular stimulation indirectly enhances synaptic transmission of thalamocortical cells, through a process of disinhibition"[12] and basal forebrain neurons are driven by brain stem reticular neurons.[13]

Can percepts exist without awareness? Even more troublesome, can awareness exist without awareness of itself? This question—the obverse of whether there can be consciousness without awareness—is equally difficult to explore: in part because it is a manifestation of a semantic problem and in part because the measuring tools are lacking. If behavior constitutes the criterion of measurement, the semantic problem is exposed; for if we agree that the isolated spinal cord that responds is not aware of the stimulus, how can the behavioral response to subliminal cortical stimuli be called awareness? In the presence of certain cerebral lesions, galvanic skin resistance studies suggest awareness despite denial of awareness. Reduplicative paramnesia (Capgras syndrome) and prosopagnosia are cases in point. In each, familiar people or faces are not recognized at the level of conscious awareness (as verbally reported), but if galvanic skin resistance is used as a measurement, awareness at a foreconscious level occurs. Autotopagnosia—the denial of ownership of an existing body part (that is, the lack of awareness of it *as* a part of the body)—includes consciousness (for it is moved spontaneously) without awareness. And its obverse—perceptual awareness without consciousness of it—exists in the phantom limb syndrome, in which an amputee may be aware of pain in a foot that does not actually exist. This is not to minimize the value of many psychological tests that demonstrate the existence of unconscious perception. These tests, however, whether in the normal or the neurologically impaired, all suffer constraints imposed by the test situation.

Often referred to in discussions of consciousness without awareness is *blindsight*. I have never understood the fascination with this oxymoron. It is but an instantiation of the hierarchical organization of the visual system, which, in turn, is an instantiation of the hierarchical organization of the nervous system on both input and output sides. This can be demonstrated if behavior is used as the instrument of measurement. From the hemianopic field, illuminate the retina of a patient with postgeniculate blindness and the pupil contracts (behavior). Does the subject see or not? At some level the nervous system "sees." It simply depends on how one defines "sees." Is elicitation of behavior enough? Pointing (for example) to objects in the hemianopic ("blind") field is behavior at the next level; does the subject see or not? Galvanic skin resistance (electrodermal behavior induced by the sweat glands) in visual agnosia is at a higher level; does the subject see or not? Verbal reporting (behavior) of a visual stimulus by a subject in an experimental or natural setting is the next level; does the subject see or not? Revisualization in the absence of an objective stimulus is the next level; do we call this seeing or not? Only in pregeniculate blindness is there no "seeing" (as judged by behavior), and, even there, we cannot be sure, for we may be employing the wrong measuring device. Remember that there are cells in the retina that respond to light even though they are not part of the *visual* system. This hierarchy is not limited to the visual system. Contraction of the stapedius muscle—to dampen the excursion of the stapes before a loud noise is heard—is the analog of the pupillary response. Did the subject hear or not? So much for starting to run before the athlete *hears* the starting gun. Crick deals with this phenomenon by postulating an "On Line System" in the case of vision.[14] This hypothetical system is simple: it produces stereotype responses, responds rapidly, and is not conscious (that is, it functions without awareness, for, in the general sense, the subject is conscious). How much more economical it is to ascribe this to low-level systems, which (because of fewer synapses) function rapidly. It was long thought, for example, that the monosynaptic myotatic knee-jerk reflex occurred too rapidly to be explained by neural connections, but we now know that the speed of the response is occasioned by its being a monosynaptic arc. In the case of hearing, the brain stem olivocochlear bundle feeds back to the peripheral cochlea to inhibit transmission to the cochlear nucleus—inhibition at a very early stage in the neural chain.

The best that can be done for the moment is to argue that consciousness evolves below the cerebral level but requires hemispheric (including subcortical nuclei and diencephalon) participation to be expressed. When the cortex is partially suppressed, as in some stages of sleep, consciousness is present, but it too is partially suppressed. In other stages of sleep, when the cortex is less suppressed, consciousness also is less suppressed. The argument is structured this way for clarity, but it should really be stated the other way around. It is not that partial suppression of cortical function causes partial suppression of consciousness but rather that altered activity of the brain stem ascending reticular activating system—or partial suppression of consciousness—causes the partial suppression of the cortical function we call sleep.

Input from the brain stem reticular formation is not in itself the criterion for the appearance of consciousness. It is necessary, but it is not sufficient. Witness the input from brain stem to spinal cord by way of facilitatory and inhibitory pathways (not all of which are reticular in origin). These pathways function to modulate the behavioral response at the spinal level, but they do not induce consciousness in the usually understood sense. Brain stem reticular formation, therefore, is necessary for the elaboration of consciousness but requires effectors of a special type (the spinal cord is not one such) in order to be expressed. These effectors are cerebral in location, are probably modular in structure, and are organized in assemblies. A cell assembly, as Hebb defined it, is "a diffuse structure comprising cells in the cortex and diencephalon . . . capable of acting briefly as a closed system."[15] These assemblies subserve two functions: one specific, such as perceptual, and a second nonspecific, such as consciousness.

Input from the brain stem reticular formation is not in itself the criterion for the appearance of consciousness.

It is reasonable to suppose that general principles of organization describe the structure and function of the nervous system. Principles apply as well to the organization of the individual systems—such as the so-called motor, sensory, and perceptual systems—that in aggregate comprise the nervous system. The principles that describe one system need not be the principles that describe another, just as the principles describing the behavior of a neuron differ from those describing the behavior of an assembly of neurons. The serially organized, hierarchical systems operate in parallel, one with the other. "The critical notion is that there is a stage at which information processing becomes integrated and serial. . . . At earlier stages the processing is carried out by distributed specialized processors which can operate in parallel, but where the response is not automatic information must be integrated so as to determine the appropriate response. At this stage processing is serial. . . . "[16] Thus processing in sensory and motor systems is serial; information is represented, re-represented, and re-re-represented, which allows for elaboration beyond cortical primary projection areas. But operating in parallel with these serial systems are other, more "automatic" systems that provide enabling support by the autonomic system, affective coloration by the limbic system, and (I suggest) receptivity and ultimately awareness by a parallel operating consciousness system. Major organizational principles that govern high-level systems include inhibition and recursion, which mature during evolutionary development. Some human systems are more evolved than others. The primitive, less evolved systems are shared by many animals. The most evolved systems are uniquely human. Thus a hierarchy of systems exists just as hierarchy exists within a given system. Motor and sensory systems are less evolved than perceptual systems, which in turn are less evolved than conceptual systems; and within systems are levels of evolution. Take, for instance, the motor system, in which the hierarchy extends from spinal function through basal nuclei to cortex. When the most elaborated organizational principles do not apply to a system, it is because that system (for example the autonomic system) has stopped evolving (that is, has fulfilled its function) at an early stage or because the system has altered its functional development by diverging.

If consciousness has evolved as the nervous system evolved, it may respond to the same principles of organization that govern other high-level components of the nervous system. These principles do not actually govern, control, or rule the systems; nor do the systems *respond* to them. The principles describe the organization that evolved. These evolutionary principles emphasize that evolution, too, is a descriptive, not explanatory, term. One strategy for studying consciousness is to analyze more readily accessible systems (such as the motor system), elucidate organizational principles, and assess how well consciousness fits the template. Is consciousness hierarchically organized? If so, have the higher levels evolved from the more primitive? Is its field of activity lateralized, as would be suggested by motor or sensory function? Are inhibition and recursion organizational principles?

This approach, which differs from those used by others, will be the avenue of exploration ahead. But, before we take that avenue, let's go on a brief meander.

Research is often conceived as a collection of beakers and flasks, a connection of microelectrodes and oscilloscopes—work at a bench. Although this is true, it has always seemed to me that research is less a pattern of performance than it is an attitude, a style of thought, or a point of view. It includes a search (which can be performed anywhere) for what lies beneath the surface. Benchwork, in most instances, can be extrapolated to the human because fundamental processes are similar across species. The structure of a protein, the mechanism of action of the heart, or the function of the liver can be studied in nonhuman animals and extended to man, because the evolutionary distance is not great. When it comes to the nervous system, however, there is a sudden ellipsis—a gap too large to bridge. Studies at the cellular level, or of early evolved systems, can be pertinent to the understanding of the human nervous system. But highly elaborated functions, such as human language, can be studied only in humans. This is particularly germane in the case of consciousness, for there are those for whom the existence of nonhuman consciousness is a question. In analyzing neurological function by looking beneath surface behavior, it is hard to avoid a structuralist viewpoint. If one accepts a Piagetian definition of a self-regulating system governed by a set of transformational rules of which the user may be unaware, behavior—and even neuronal function—can be observed from a structuralist point of view. That point of view, or attitude, can be applied in the various arenas of human activity, but is least effective (I suggest) in the special laboratory situation. Watching humans—particularly children—at work or at play tells a great deal about the functional organization of the nervous system. The clinic offers a special privilege, for here we can see various layers of neurological function exposed by destructive processes. If the research attitude is brought to the bedside, special insights nowhere else available can be obtained. In that setting, issues of human consciousness can be addressed.

To look below the surface, we will use the laboratory and the clinic. We will ask: What does a given behavior mean?, why is it happening?, and, in some broad sense, are there transformational rules that govern it?—if so, can we define as a first approximation what these rules are?

3

This They Believe: Other Views

Recent writings on consciousness—of which there has been a spate in the past decade, though only a few will be considered here—tend to fall into one of two groups: those by philosophers and those by physical scientists. The first are often based on logic and introspection. The second employ interpretation of physical events, often grafted onto preconception. In the first group are Searle, Dennett, Chalmers, and Honderich. In the second group are Crick, Koch, and Hobson. Then there are some, such as Edelman, who span both groups. Because their methods differ, the conclusions of the two groups often differ. On occasion, it even seems they are not participating in the same arena.

Some of the evidence presented by the physical scientists is reductionist. Neural activity is studied at the cellular level or in small groups of cells, but systems are ignored. How to relate the reductionist data to systems or organisms is not explored. At the other extreme, function is ascribed to places, just as, in the time of Descartes, the seat of the soul was placed in the unpaired pineal body (because it was unpaired). Perhaps it should come as no surprise that Crick's *The Scientific Search for the Soul*, despite its cellular emphasis, ends up localizing consciousness as if it (or the soul, or the will) were a thing. Libet, too, searches for the soul, but at least he believes "self and soul are emergent phenomena of brain activity."[1] Localization works well for the clinical neurologist whose aim (before the days of computed tomography) was to localize the site of a lesion. Often this could be done with great precision by the experienced practitioner, who, it was to be hoped, did not localize the absent function at the locus of the lesion. That the lesion interrupted a function did not mean the function was located there. That trap was to be assiduously avoided, but many got caught nevertheless. That a left temporal lesion produces aphasia does not mean language is located in the left temporal lobe—but who could bother to remember that?

So, when Crick tells us the thalamus is a "key player in consciousness," with information flowing in several directions at once (shades of Penfield's centrencephalon), one hopes he is not telling us that consciousness is located there. He writes, "Each particular thalamic region may handle its own form of attention, possibly by allowing neurons in its member set of cortical areas to talk to neurons in the thalamus, which in turn feed back to them, so that in some way their firing is coordinated."[2] If this is a localization of a function, it is an old-fashioned view for a sophisticated scientist to adopt. However, other of Crick's comments suggest localizationism. Take, for example, his discussion of free will. Because I don't know if he was feigning ignorance to provoke an antagonist, I will let him speak for himself. "Where, I wondered, might Free Will be located in the brain? . . . I went over to tea one day and announced to Pat Churchland and Terry Sejnowski that the seat of the Will had been discovered! It was at or near the anterior cingulate."[3] This, based in part on a description of a case of a woman with a lesion in the anterior cingulate, sounds very much like localization of a function based on its absence. Perhaps this was irony, but not all of his readers recognized it.

The problem of localization, however determined (loss of function following a cerebral lesion, increased blood flow on imaging studies, or electrophysiological activity), is that it conflates three entities that, in a disciplined analysis, must remain distinct. I emphasize again that the localization of a lesion by clinical (loss of function), anatomic (imaging), or physiological (electroencephalographic) methods is different from locating a function at the site of the lesion. The three entities that need to be sharply separated are place, process, and property. The place is anatomical: a morphological location in the brain that may include connections to distant regions not demonstrable by customary techniques. The process is neural: the activity of nerve cells, fibers, and synapses. The property is what emerges from the functioning of specific assemblies of neural modules. The three are related—perhaps even causally—but they are different from each other and the distinction must be honored. Thus to say "sensorimotor intentions are located in the posterior parietal cortex"[4] or "free will" is located "at or near the anterior cingulate"[5, 6] represents an unwarranted merging of the three levels of analysis. Nor is the situation rectified by Pockett's claim that "the notion that intentions are 'located' in the posterior parietal cortex may annoy some philosophers, but the word is chosen quite deliberately. Intentions in this sense are not abstract entities—they are patterns of neural activity; or perhaps patterns of synaptic strength which are eventually played out into patterns of neural activity. Either kind of pattern clearly has both temporal and spatial extension, which means it must be located somewhere."[7] To me, intention is no more located in nerves than is pain or vision. As I see it, the neural activity must be located somewhere—namely, in the nerves. The nerves must be located somewhere—namely, in a region of the brain. And the product emerging from the pattern must be located somewhere—or must it? This property (call it transitive consciousness) is a function widely distributed—an emergent property—and cannot be localized except in the most general way. It cannot be placed in a specific (both senses) area. Isn't that the problem? If it were like vision or somatic sensation (and even those modalities cannot be sharply localized), we would have less difficulty dealing with it.

This flavor of localizationism appears again in Koch (a close collaborator of Crick), who accepts the term *essential node* to describe a "damaged portion of the brain for that particular conscious attribute."[8] He, as did Crick, ascribes a function to a location on the basis of its absence secondary to a lesion—a logical fallacy. The importance of this localizationist approach is that Koch extends it (if I understand him correctly) to his Neuronal Correlate of Consciousness (NCC), which he *localizes* in the "upper region of the ventral vision-for-perception pathway," some of whose "members are the most promising candidates for the NCC."[9] This localization contrasts with the view that representation of consciousness is widely distributed—and, when taken in conjunction with the notion of essential node, suggests that a lesion in a temporal lobe would impair or destroy consciousness. That does not occur, even if the temporal lobe lesion is bilateral.

To worsen matters, the ambiguity of Koch's language makes it unclear whether this localized function is bilateral or is a unilateral dominant function (in the sense that he relates a dominant hemisphere to language). So when he writes that "the NCC must employ the callosal fibers to establish a single, *dominant* coalition throughout the forebrain," is this coalition unilaterally or bilaterally based?[10] Nor does the recapitulation of "integrate neural activity in the two halves of the forebrain, such that only a single dominant coalition forms," help to clarify.[11] In this formulation, the dominant forebrain coalition feeds back to the coalitions of the ventral visual pathways a hierarchical view that would accord well with the hierarchical organization of much of the cerebral cortex—but "we don't even know if this sector of the brain is organized along hierarchical lines."[12]

Hierarchical lines raise again the issue of principles, rules, or laws, so a point to stress once more is the distinction that must be made between the neural process and the emergent property. Each is governed by principles (that is, described by rules), which probably vary. As Searle says: "The neuron firings cause the feeling, but they are not the same thing as the feeling."[13] It is difficult, therefore, for me to understand his controversy with Chalmers, who feels the need for a third set of rules. "So to explain why and how brains support consciousness an account of the brain alone is not enough; to bridge the gap, one needs to add independent 'bridging' laws."[14] "The principle of structural coherence allows us to understand what is going on. In essence, this principle is being used as a *background assumption* to provide a bridge from features of the physical processes to features of the experience" (italics in original).[15] "If we take for granted the coherence between the structure of consciousness and the structure of awareness, then, in order to explain some specific aspect of the former, we need only explain the corresponding aspect of the latter. The bridging principle does the rest of the work."[16] These bridging laws would only describe the transition from the neural to the conscious in an orderly, systematic way. Obviously, we don't know them yet. We don't even know if they exist. But the idea of bridging laws is credible unless one argues that the neural activity itself is consciousness or feeling. Perhaps Searle's objection is semantic, for there is no pain in the neuronal substrate of conscious pain. Is that what he means when he writes, "There is no meaning of the word 'pain,' for example, where for every conscious pain in the world there must be a correlated nonconscious functional state which is called 'pain'"?[17]

The merging of consciousness with awareness allows Crick to say: "Consciousness takes many forms," and "Koch and I chose visual awareness rather than other forms of consciousness, such as pain or self-consciousness," thereby extending what I would view as the specific member of the duo through three input levels (sensation, perception, and conceptualization) as forms of consciousness.[18]

This kind of fuzzy border recurs when Koch says: "These *sensory* qualities, the building blocks of conscious experience have traditionally been called *qualia*" (*qualia* italicized in the original, *sensory* italics added).[19] Many problems arise in this one sentence. Surely we should draw a sharp boundary between a sensory experience and its quality;

Surely we should draw a sharp boundary between a sensory experience and its quality

seeing red (to use Crick's example)—which is a sensation—is rather different from the redness of red—a quale. Next, are sensory experiences, or even qualia (two different entities), the building blocks of consciousness? Or are they the building blocks of experience? Honderich suggests not; writing of qualia he says: "Very evidently not the character of all consciousness" and, later, "not the general nature of perceptual consciousness," which might be interpreted as experience.[20] For Searle: "Conscious experiences have a qualitative aspect," but this does not suggest the quale is a building block of consciousness; however, it does suggest the quale relates to the experience, not to the consciousness.[21] Searle makes other important contributions that help delineate the distinction between consciousness and the experience of a modality (although I don't think he shares what might be called my *strong* view). He writes in three separate places: "Perception of the sort Koch is investigating does not create consciousness but modifies a preexisting conscious field."[22] Later in this review of Koch's book he writes: "The problem is that he does not consider the possibility that the existence of the unified conscious field may be an 'enabling condition' for the various building blocks that he studies."[23] The enabling conditions are factors Koch distinguishes from the specific factors: "Enabling factors are tonic conditions and systems that are needed for any form of consciousness to occur at all, while specific factors are required for any one particular conscious concept."[24] His specific factors may result from input by the specific systems (in the anatomic sense). His enabling factors (he calls them NCC_e) embrace two categories: one neural, and one constitutional. That general bodily functions (such as blood supply) are enabling is a truism. The neural category is not enabling for consciousness but rather for the percept. It is not NCC_e but really NCC, which is defined as a: "Temporary subset of particular neurons in the cortical thalamic system whose firing is synchronized,"[25] or, alternatively, as: "The minimal set of neuronal events and mechanisms jointly sufficient for a specific conscious percept."[26] This category of enabling factors forces him to ask, "Is it possible to be conscious without being conscious of anything in particular? That is, can NCC_e be present without any NCC?"[27] And this question compels consideration of the mesencephalic reticular formation. He identifies it, acknowledges its function as an ascending activating system, and discusses its distribution and its transmitters. He tips his hat in passing, but will not say hello. Only reluctantly does he admit: "Without the influence of the brainstem and thalamic nuclei, an organism cannot be conscious of anything. . . . [T]hey are enablers but not content providers. That is the job of the cortex and the thalamus."[28] Taking his first reference to the thalamus to be to the nonspecific intralaminar nuclei, and his second reference to be to the specific thalamic nuclei, what better division could one ask for the distinction of consciousness and awareness (or perception)? But he will not acknowledge this separation; as late as page 320 (and again in the glossary) he merges the two: "Interviewer: Wait. Why do you say 'awareness' instead of 'consciousness'? Do they refer to different concepts? Christof: No. It is more of a social convention. Consciousness—the C word—evokes powerful aversive reactions in some colleagues; so you are better off with some other word in grant applications and journal submissions. 'Awareness' usually slips under the radar."[29] So much for grant applications, journal articles, and peer review. But I fear something else has also eluded the radar. Why not accept Searle's point: "In my view we will not understand consciousness until we understand how the brain creates the conscious field to begin with"?[30] The evidence is all there, but the acknowledgment is grudging. Speaking of brain stem and thalamic intralaminar nuclei, Koch admits that "These nuclei therefore lack the basic infrastructure to support the content of stimulus and awareness."[31] The crucial word here is *awareness*. He then distinguishes this awareness from consciousness (despite his equation in many other places) by continuing: "Without the ascending influence of the brain-stem and thalamic nuclei"—remember, he is speaking of the intralaminar thalamic nuclei—"an organism cannot be consciousness of anything."[32] There it is—but he won't keep them separate.[33]

Hobson, too, acknowledges and denies. "The *level* of consciousness is set by an internal electrochemical drive system that has been called the 'nonspecific reticular activating system'"[34] (italics in the original). And then, paradoxically, "Activation of the brain is automatically maintained at a high level even when we are unconscious," meaning asleep.[35]

Among the philosophers, Chalmers has a special way of handling the consciousness-awareness twin. He distinguishes two concepts of mind: the phenomenal and the psychological. The phenomenal is "the concept of mind as conscious experience and of a mental state as a consciously experienced mental state," or what I would construe as conscious awareness and self-consciousness respectively.[36] The psychological concept of mind is "the causal or explanatory basis for behavior."[37] He then goes on to identify awareness as "the most general brand of psychological consciousness."[38] He allows that many mental concepts (perception, for example) partake of both. The combination of the psychological and phenomenal exists: "It is natural to suppose there might be a psychological property associated with experience itself, or with phenomenal consciousness."[39] But that suggests the two are separate, a view supported by his statement that, although the psychological and phenomenal occur together, "they should not be conflated." If awareness is psychological and should not be conflated with the phenomenal, it is separable. And the phenomenal, in which "mind is characterized by the way it *feels*" (italics in the original), has overtones of limbic and reticular substrates.[40]

For Damasio (in Metzinger), the structures necessary for the operation of consciousness are located near the midline and in the depth of the brain, but "the neocortical regions . . . are also involved in the process of making consciousness."[41] These first order structures, "the early sensory cortices are involved in processing separate aspects of objects and the disabling of one of these regions, even if extensive, does not compromise the central resource of consciousness but only a sector of it."[42] For me, the sector loss at this level is of the percept. A sector of consciousness may also be lost but is not demonstrable, because it is overridden by the loss of percept. But he continues: "On the other hand, the regions that support the protoself, and second order structures constitute a central resource, and their dysfunction causes a disruption of the process of consciousness."[43] These second order structures map (remap) what goes on in the first order map, which maps the relation of the object and the organism. These I view as sensory or perceptual representations of the object, to which the organism responds. The reiteration in his second order structures—what I consider conceptual or cognitive derivatives of first order input—is essential to consciousness in his formation. *"Consciousness is constituted by the images that these second-order maps contribute to the mind, in the form of a sense of self knowing"* (italics in the original).[44] It is loss here, rather than at the first order level, that I visualize as a loss of a sector of consciousness demonstrable in an agnosia for an agnosia (courage . . . keep going). What of the protoself? This is a nonconscious representation of "the state of the living body in its many dimensions."[45] It is responsible for homeostasis: "the relative stability required for survival."[46] The neural devices necessary to support the protoself include brain stem nuclei, hypothalamus, basal forebrain, and insula. One might have anticipated the ascending reticular activating system to appear here, but the exclusion is specific because "consciousness can be separated from wakefulness and low-level attention"[47] although his "conclusions do not deny that some brainstem structures are involved in the process of wakefulness and attention, and that they modulate the activity of cerebral cortex via the intralaminar thalamic nuclei, the non-thalamic cortical projections of monamines, and the thalamic projections of acetylcholine nuclei."[48]

Libet approaches the topic of consciousness from the vantage of a physiologist. He extrapolates from his work on evoked potentials (EP), also called event-related potentials (ERP), and the readiness potential (RP) that precedes voluntary action. Evoked potentials appear over an appropriate area of cerebral cortex (somatosensory, visual, and auditory) in response to sensory stimuli and can be recorded from the scalp or, during surgery, from exposed cortex. When stimuli are below threshold for awareness, a primary evoked potential is not followed by late components. These late components correlate with awareness, an "emergent result of appropriate neuronal activities where these persist for a minimum duration of up to 0.5 sec."[49] The evoked potential serves as a marker in time to which the delayed awareness is referred. This delayed awareness is ascribed to the late event-related potential. It is known that in the somatosensory system all events up to and including P14 are generated below the thalamus. (P and N refer to polarity of deflection—positive or negative—and the numerals indicate time to peak in milliseconds; thus P14 is a positive deflection at 14 ms). The first cortical component is N20. Early components of event-related potentials are unchanged with manipulation of attention. Amplitude of the P40, N60, P100, and P300 is increased with attention to somesthetic stimuli.[50]

Awareness, in Libet's study, is defined by an introspective report. "The only valid evidence of subjective awareness is an introspective report of awareness."[51] Using the introspective report as the operational criterion, however, introduces a complication, for what is being reported is actually awareness of awareness; there is also unconscious awareness that the subject is unaware of and therefore does not report. The correlation of the late event-related potential with reported awareness does not in itself imply a causal relation. The neural "cause" may be generated elsewhere. This should be testable. Libet says, "the *later* response of the cerebral cortex, produced after a *single pulse to the skin* appears to be necessary for producing a conscious sensation" (italics in the original).[52] Imagine an experiment in which a single pulse to the skin is, or is not, delivered during a specified period of time. For each specified period of time (say one minute on a clock viewed by the subject), the subject is to report awareness of whether the stimulus was, or was not, delivered. When delivered, the cortical response would include late event-related potentials, and awareness would be reported. When not delivered, the cortical response presumably would not include late event-related potentials, but the reported response of the subject who was unaware of the (absent) stimulus would be awareness of unawareness generated by something other than the ERP. In fact, this experiment may have been done already if subjects who received subliminal stimuli reported the lack of feeling—an awareness of unawareness in the absence of late ERP. The proposed experiment would not address directly whether the late event-related potentials are necessary for awareness, but it would address whether ERP was necessary for awareness of awareness or of unawareness. It would also speak to the potential pitfall in using an introspective verbal report as a criterion for awareness. It is known that an omitted stimulus can illicit an ERP (P300), but this occurs in a long train of repeated stimuli, not in response to a single stimulus. In this sense, the readiness potential, which precedes a voluntary act (RP, decision to act, action), could be viewed as a decision to decide (Libet's RPi—preplanned, decision to decide, RPii—not preplanned, decision). This potential originates in the supplementary motor area for self-generated movement and specifies particular movements. Studies in monkeys show "that if monkeys perform different sequences of movements, where there is no external cue to specify which movements to make, there are cells in the SMA" (supplementary motor area) "that fire before one sequence but not before the others."[53]

So far Libet's conclusions have been based on empirical evidence. When he proceeds to the postulate of a "conscious mental field" (a field in the sense of, but distinct from, physical fields such as electromagnetic or gravitational) as the "mediator between the physical activities of nerve cells and the emergence of subjective experience," he moves into areas of speculation (which is allowable) that are reminiscent of dualism.[54] He writes, "Activation of a cortical area can contribute to overall unified conscious experience by some mode other than by neural messages delivered via nerve conduction."[55] By means of the proposed field theory, "a cortical area can contribute to or affect the larger conscious field."[56] Libet is clearly aware of the overtones of dualism, for he says, "the CMF is proposed as a 'property' of an emergent phenomenon of the brain. The CMF is clearly not in the separate substance category of Cartesian dualism. The CMF does not exist without the brain. It emerges from the appropriate system of neural activities."[57] For the moment, this simply introduces another layer in the correspondence between the neural and the mental.

Many sophisticated, technologically advanced methods are used by physical scientists. These include microelectrode studies, computer generation of stimuli, and functional imaging by magnetic resonance or positron emission.[58] The techniques vary in method and in level of exploration, but they have in common one factor that unites them. They are all *tests* administered in artificially (that is, nonbiologically) structured situations. "Whereas the goals of action are set in the laboratory by the instructions given, in the everyday world they are set by the goals that people set for themselves."[59]

It has always seemed to me that a great conceptual step forward was taken in biology when the frog's retinal ganglion cell was identified as a bug receptor rather than as a neuron responding to a moving stimulus. That step on the response side was not paralleled on the stimulus side, for we are only partly aware that the computer-generated moving stimulus is not a bug (not even a simulated bug), but a pretend bug. For a response it requires a nervous system able, at some level, to pretend. This is a high-level function, and, if present, the nervous system may choose not to use it. The response, like the Emergency Broadcast Signal, may be "this is a test . . . this is only a test." And, like the response to the Emergency Broadcast Signal, the organism may do nothing. Or, should the nervous system decide to participate in the test, its response may be "this is not a pipe, it is only a picture of a pipe." After all, as I am told, the Korean proverb reads, "You cannot eat the picture of a meal."

That this excursion is not mere carping becomes evident in agnosia, in which the biological significance of the stimulus determines its adequacy. But the biological significance of the stimulus is determined by more than just the nature of the stimulus. It includes the state of the organism (hungry or not), the internal and external context in which it is presented, and the accumulated experience of the respondent. What is biologically significant on one occasion may not be so on another.

Conclusions drawn by scientists on the basis of these physical techniques are clearly of importance but must be used with caution. Because a neuron or an assembly of neurons participates in a process, the conclusion may not be drawn that it is either responsible for, or the site of, a function—the spark plug analogy once again. That neuron or assembly may be a participant in or an accompaniment to the process; or it may be a base on which the process under study (but also many other processes) can be placed. This, then, is part of the problem confronting those who study consciousness only by physical techniques.

Among the philosophers, Dennett raises some special problems in an area shared by other philosophers. He talks of sentience as "the more or less standard term for what is imagined to be the lowest grade of consciousness."[60] The definition of sentience in the *Oxford English Dictionary*—which may not be what the philosophers have in mind— raises an exciting possibility. For the *OED*, sentience is "susceptibility to sensation." For me, that suggests that it is present in the absence of sensation, can occur in conjunction with sensation, and may be an analog of the "lowest grade of consciousness" created by the brain stem ascending reticular activating system. No such luck. Having given us that (yellow leaves), Dennett takes the lowest grade of conscious back (or none) to return a small amount later (or few). "Everyone agrees that sentience requires sensitivity" (does he mean sensation?) "plus some further as yet unidentified factor."[61]

On this point Searle is of no help. He describes consciousness (it can hardly be called a definition, despite his statement that "it does not seem to me that consciousness is hard to define"): "Consciousness consists of states of awareness or sentience or feeling."[62] The problems this presents are threefold: (1) It does not separate conscious awareness into its two components. Much experimental and clinical data suggest that consciousness and awareness are separable. (2) It does not indicate whether sentience is a "susceptibility," as suggested by the *OED*, and generated by the brain stem ascending reticular activating system, or a "power or function of sensation or perception by the senses," as the *OED* suggests for "sentient." If the latter, then it is presumably mediated by a separate neurological system—the lemniscal system—from sentience as a readiness or activation only. (3) It is not clear whether by "feeling" he means somatic sensation (general or special in the terms of the anatomist), or emotional states. I suspect the latter. If so, and if limbic cortex is considered important in the genesis of emotional states (without the implication of intentionality), the interesting possibility arises that the limbic system participates in the production of consciousness, which is a view not usually considered. What makes this speculation appealing relates to the newborn and the very young infant. Three questions might be asked about this early life period before many areas of cerebral cortex have yet to develop fully: (1) Is the newborn conscious? Most answer yes. During this period limbic cortex functions, but visual cortex (to cite a region of interest in the discussion of consciousness) has not matured. Morgan notes: "The smiles come very early, within days of birth."[63] (2) Is the newborn aware? If so, of what? Most would agree, I believe, that awareness is limited, largely confined to sensations from the body, not to percepts from the outside world. These body sensations are brought to awareness by thalamic (pain) and limbic (pleasure/displeasure) regions. (3) Is the newborn self-conscious? Most would argue no. Awareness is limited and awareness of awareness nonexistent. Hobson considers newborns in possession of only "five of the nine components of primary consciousness"[64] and quotes Kagan's postulate that "consciousness emerges gradually during the second year of human life and culminates at about age 2."[65]

What accounts for this parcellation of consciousness in the newborn? Surely it relates somehow to the brain—and, most reasonably, to its maturation or development. But the brain does not mature all at once. A system has its own schedule of development, which may differ considerably from the timetable of a different system. "Studies in human infants show that virtually all cortical functions, including language, have anlage in early infancy and do not arise de novo at a late stage of maturation."[66] The potential is there, waiting to be put to use. But "The integration of sensory, motor, limbic and associative areas occurs *pari passu* with the structural development of the cortex as a unified structure" (italics in original).[67] This integration can be achieved in multimodal regions in which a given neuron will respond to input by more than one modality; simultaneous input of several modalities may elicit a greater response (spike frequency) than the sum of the individual inputs. These polysensory regions (in cortex and superior colliculus) serve to link immediate behavior with the "perceptual and cognitive processes that coincide with these behaviors and provide conscious dimension to the experience."[68] Some contend that synesthesia is normal for the newborn—that sensation is a primitive unity—but synesthesia means the appreciation of one modality as another (sound producing pain, for example) without the necessary implication of multimodal (rather than cross modal) registration. So, for example, imaging studies show greater participation of visual cortex in response to somatosensory tasks on the part of the early blind than of control groups. Using the cat superior colliculus neurons as a model, the incidence of multisensory neurons increases in the postnatal period, becoming greatest in adulthood.[69] Perhaps consideration should be given to the possibility that consciousness in the intransitive sense is present at birth but requires development of multimodal cells (and regions) to appear in the transitive sense, for awareness of the environment is multimodal.

To pursue this speculation to another level, if "*conscious awareness of unconsciously monitored* actions is the means by which . . . consciousness is thus embodied" (italics in the original), then the neurons that mirror the action of others without overt associated movement of the self may relate to self-consciousness.[70] These "mirror neurons are at the basis of action."[71] Located in the frontal, parietal, and superior temporal regions, these visually stimulated nerve cells seem to respond to the meaning of an action, and not only to vision but also to sound (echoneurons). They have been postulated as important in the evolution of language from gesture. If self-consciousness requires an internal symbol system for its existence, language (in some form) is an outstanding candidate. In humans, mirror neurons code for means as well as for ends. They reflect the action (in macaques) of others or "when the agent does the same type of act herself"[72] and are thought to account for "understanding the mental states that motivate the actions of others."[73] If they reflect the actions of self and the motivations of the actions of others, these cells, residing in the evolutionarily late-developed cortex, warrant consideration as the substrate for self-consciousness.

Dennett pursues sentience—his "lowest grade of consciousness"—one step further. "Sentience," he writes, "comes in every imaginable grade or intensity, from the simplest and most 'robotic' to the most exquisitely sensitive, hyper-reactive 'human'."[74] Giving us the "robotic," even in the special sense in which he uses it, means a lack of awareness, for he writes about the robotic: "Does that mean that such macromolecules have minds like ours? Certainly not. They're not even alive. They're just huge crystals, from the point of view of chemistry. These gigantic molecules are tiny machines—*macro*molecular, *nano*technology. They are in effect natural robots" (original italics).[75] So, once again, the analogy with the brain stem ascending reticular activating system is raised. This is important because he goes on in the next sentence to state that "we do indeed have to draw lines across this multi-stranded continuum of cases" (I understand this continuum to be from the most robotic to the most sensitive human) "because having moral policies requires it, but the prospect that we will *discover* a threshold—a morally significant 'step' in what is otherwise a ramp—is not only extremely unlikely but morally unappealing as well" (original italics).[76]

If in the human, the lowest level of consciousness is generated by the brain stem ascending reticular activating system, and if it corresponds to his "lowest grade of consciousness"—called sentience—which is present in the "most robotic," there is no point in looking for a threshold in the continuum ramp from robotic to human. Consciousness, constructed of nonconsciousness elements, crossed that threshold before the robotic. After that, consciousness evolves slowly along a metaphorical ascending ramp. It is the prerobotic threshold that allows an aggregation of nonconsciousness elements to become the sentience of the robotic. What makes this whole discussion pointless is that Dennett's "robotic" in his special sense is given sentience—his lowest grade of consciousness—but is described as without minds: not alive: "These impersonal, unreflective, robotic, mindless little scraps of molecular machinery are the ultimate basis of all the agency, and hence meaning, and hence consciousness, in the world."[77] If they are without conscious-ness, then, by definition, there must be a threshold (consciousness pres-ent on one side, not on the other) along the ramp. Or if, as stated elsewhere, the robotic has sentience, the threshold must be prerobotic. But it can't be both ways—sentient or mindless scraps—unless this is some form of panpsychism.

The aggregation of nonconsciousness elements to produce the lowest level of consciousness is given (as Koch gave it) only token acknowledg-ment by most philosophers. They may allow the existence of a back-ground state or field, but they do not construe it as consciousness until it becomes coupled with awareness—a cortical function. This is surprising because a distinction was recognized as long ago as antiquity (although not with reference to the ascending reticular activating system). Aristotle writes "we use the word 'perceive' in two ways, for we say (a) that what has the power to hear or see, 'sees' or 'hears,' even though it is at the moment asleep, and also (b) that what is actually seeing or hearing 'sees' or 'hears.' Hence, sense, too, must have two meanings, sense potential and sense actual. Similarly 'to be sentient' means either (a) to have a cer-tain power or (b) to manifest a certain activity."[78] His reference to "power" or "potential" as distinct from "actual" or "activity"—and his interesting reference to sleep—is the very distinction I find present in the "readiness" or consciousness component and the awareness or perceptual contribu-tion. Perhaps this reluctance of modern philosophers relates to the lack of a clear term other than "sentience" for this low level of consciousness, a state I think of as readiness to respond at a cerebral level to stimuli, a state analogous to vigilance in the attention system. We could call it "con-sciousable"—that is, able to be conscious—but more important than a neologism is an awareness of its existence. It is this low-level component of the consciousness hierarchy, this sentience in the *OED* phrasing of "susceptibility to sensation," that allows the distinction of clinical uncon-sciousness from a state of sleep. The sleeper can be roused (is suscepti-ble to sensation), but the clinically unconscious organism cannot (although it may still be susceptible to some sensations). If vigilance in the attention system corresponds to this readiness in the consciousness system (and the two systems may share a common substrate) then focused attention can be construed as the analog of perceptual aware-ness via the thalamic-specific system. This allows the speculation that the gating activity of the reticular nucleus of the thalamus on the specific nuclei of the thalamus is the Broadbent attention filter.

Of the modern philosophers, Chalmers (in Metzinger) is perhaps the most explicit in recognizing the distinction between consciousness and awareness (of a percept or sensation), but even he fails to draw a sharp line. Speaking of work on visual consciousness he says, it "is not concerned merely with the neural states that determine that one *has* visual consciousness; it is concerned with the neural states that determine the specific contents of visual consciousness" (original italics)—specific contents conveyed by a specific system.[79] I suspect a close relation between his content and his phenomenal properties—"in essence the property of having a conscious experience of that kind," understanding experience to imply contents.[80] So, his statement that "if we could then find a neural system whose states do not arbitrarily correlate with the phenomenal states in question, but vary along a corresponding systematic dimension then the NCC in question will have much greater explanatory and predictive power" suggests the division into specific and nonspecific systems and a separation of consciousness from awareness.[81] But that interpretation is less than secure in light of his subsequent distinction "between the neural correlates of background state of consciousness (wakefulness, dreaming, etc.) and the neural correlate of specific contents," because the background state—certainly dreaming—includes awareness of contents.[82]

Edelman is perhaps the most generous in acknowledging the consciousness aspect of the arousal system. He writes that "there are different levels of consciousness. In rapid eye movement (REM) sleep, for example, dreams are conscious states . . . in deep or slow-wave sleep, short dreamlike episodes may occur, but for long periods there is no evidence of consciousness"—no evidence of consciousness to the observer and to the subject, that is.[83] The outside observer does well to recall the all-too-familiar apothegm: "Absence of evidence is not evidence of absence." The objective observer is not poised to make a judgment about the consciousness of another if, as all agree, consciousness is a subjective state. And, ironically, even the subject is not poised to make a judgment about consciousness in slow-wave sleep. The lack of memory, on waking, of a subjective state during slow-wave sleep is a manifestation of memory, not of consciousness; and it may be no different from the difficulty recalling the dreams of REM sleep, which is accepted as a conscious state. Even Hobson, for whom consciousness is awareness, writes that "we already know that low levels of waking conscious experience persist even in very deep NREM sleep."[84] Perhaps the commonplace notion of "sleeping on it" should be reexamined. You take a problem to bed. You wake with it solved. There is no recollection of grappling with it during the night. There is no awareness of having dealt with it. But something must have been going on. Better to be viewed as consciousness without awareness than as unconsciousness.

Despite his generosity, Edelman's emphasis is on the specific contributions to consciousness, and on occasion he ignores entirely the simultaneously active nonspecific component, writing that "Consciousness is itself an internally constructed phenomenon. By this I mean that, although perceptual input is important initially, in relatively short order the brain can go beyond the information given, or even (as in REM sleep) create conscious scenes without input from or output to the external world."[85] And yet that REM sleep—as well as, I believe, the base on which to establish perceptual and conceptual aspects of consciousness—is generated initially in the brain stem.

Flohr (in Metzinger) offers an explicit mechanism for the activity of the brain stem ascending reticular activating system. Discussing the N-methyl-D aspartate receptor, he notes (on the basis of the effects of drugs) the receptors' importance in maintenance of consciousness.[86] The opening of the ion channel of these receptors is both voltage- and transmitter-dependent. Presynaptic glutamate must be released, and the postsynaptic membrane must be depolarized to about -35 mV. The question of why diffuse activation of the cortex is necessary for consciousness is analyzed in the context of the NMDA receptor. Flohr suggests the arousal state generated by the brain stem ascending reticular activating system adjusts the potential of the postsynaptic membrane in which the NMDA receptor is imbedded. "Only if this potential is kept near the threshold of the activation of this receptor will these synapses participate in cortical information processing. The unspecific activation of the cortical neurons determines the rate at which the NMDA-dependent processes take place. A minimum activation of cortical NDMA system is a necessary condition for the mechanism's underlying consciousness." He also points out that "Discrete unilateral lesions of the ascending pathways lead to focal disturbances of consciousness, such as attentional neglect," raising again the relation of attention to consciousness.[87]

Dehaene and colleagues suggest, "Ascending brainstem nuclei (e.g. cholinergic among others) send globally depolarizing neuromodulatory signals to a thalamic and cortical hierarchy. Simulations show a progressive increase in spontaneous firing as a function of neuromodulator release, which evolves in what is known in dynamical systems theory as a Hopf bifurcation: spontaneous firing increases continuously in intensity, but high-frequency oscillations appear suddenly in the gamma band (20–80 Hz). By increasing spontaneous activity, and thus bringing a broad thalamo-cortical network closer to firing threshold, vigilance lowers the threshold for external sensory inputs."[88] Vigilance in their report is the term chosen for consciousness in the nontransitive sense. "Vigilance is a graded variable, and a minimal level is essential for placing thalamo-cortical systems into a receptive state."[89]

Without mentioning the brain stem ascending reticular activating system, Searle, by implication, seems sympathetic to the idea of something serving as fundamental for consciousness. In his discussion of the current neurobiological approaches to consciousness, he proposes the existence of two camps: One uses the "building block approach," and the other employs the "unified field approach." The building block approach really explores problems of perception rather than of consciousness, which is why the visual system is used and is often cited in discussions of consciousness. The strategy behind the building block approach, Searle writes, is this: "If we could figure out exactly how the brain causes even one building block, say the *perception of red*, then we might use that knowledge to track the whole problem of consciousness" (italics added).[90] Although—as Searle notes—this is "the approach most commonly favored by existing researchers in the field," he is partial to the unified field approach. *"We should think of perception not as creating consciousness but as modifying a pre-existing conscious field"* (original italics).[91] This could well be a description of the brain stem ascending reticular activating system, which establishes a cortical field on which to display percepts.

The "feeling" Searle ascribes to consciousness introduces the difficult area of qualia. For Searle "All conscious states are qualitative in the sense that there is something that it feels like, a qualitative feel, to be in that state. (Some authors use the word *qualia*, singular quale, to identify these qualitative experiences.)"[92] This is rather different from Koch's "qualia are the elements that make up conscious experience."[93] Humphrey equates qualia with phenomenal consciousness.[94] Qualia constitute the "essence of subjectivity," are "not thinkable, not communicable, and not *about* anything" (original italics).[95] They are not propositional, and they have no intentionality. Most important, they are the result of an action—or of what I view as an operation—of the nervous system on the environment. Qualia are generated by the subject (experient), but, unlike propositional experience (perception), they do not require an environmental stimulus (except, of course, insofar as the brain, which generates the stimulus, is part of the environment).

Edelman states this notion in two ways, each of which may be the same except that their slight difference in wording creates (for me) some ambiguities that are potentially important. He says, "The term 'quale' refers to the particular experience of some property—of greenness for instance, or warmth, or painfulness."[96] Later "the term 'quale' has been applied to the experience of feeling—say of green or warmth or pain."[97] "Feeling," which is present in the second definition, is lacking in the first, unless of course the experience of greenness is the feeling of green. Just as consciousness and awareness should be kept separate, so, I believe, the experience of some property (awareness of a percept) and the feeling (the affective accompaniment of that experience) should be kept separate. The two are separable because they are generated by two separate neurological systems (an isocortical perceptual system with its primary projection and associated areas of elaboration for the percept and separate parallel participation by the limbic system for the feeling or emotional overtone).[98]

The feeling engendered by the percept may have no relation to the percept. In fact feelings are not attributes of objects; feelings are generated within the organism and are induced by the simultaneous operation of a number of entities, among which are memory, context, and associations. Percepts, too, are generated within the organism, and they employ memory, context, and associations but differ from feeling by their need for an objective stimulus external to the nervous system.

Part of the problem results from the variable use of the term *qualia*. "Different authors use the term 'qualia' in different ways," Chalmers notes.[99] To him "A mental state is conscious if it has a *qualitative feel*— an associated quality of experience. These qualitative feels are also known as phenomenal qualities or *qualia* for short" (original italics).[100] The pivotal word here is "associated"—a quality associated with (but presumably independent of) experience or its content. This independence is strongly suggested by his statement that "Whenever one has a green sensation, individuated phenomenally, one has a corresponding green *perception* individuated psychologically" (original italics).[101] Chalmers's (and Humphrey's) use of the term "sensation" differs from the way it is understood in the input hierarchy we employ. The problem is to find an alternative term; neither "affect" nor "feeling" is quite correct, although there is something of these qualities. That "feeling" quality (referred to by Chalmers, Searle, and others) is what generates the term *quale*, raises the question of limbic participation, and distinguishes it from perception or its content. I understand his "green sensation individuated phenomenally" to be a percept (green) that has a particular feeling tone (greenness). Honderich writes of "Ideas in a certain sense or sense data, or percepts, or qualia of a kind."[102] It is not clear whether these are contrasted or identical until he binds them together twelve pages later as "so-called subjective items."[103] It is very difficult to get a crisp philosophical definition of *qualia*. That it is subjective does not distinguish it from percepts or sensations, which are also subjective. That it is a feeling never clarifies whether this means affective or sensory. Honderich's suggestion that qualia "are elusive differences between kinds of perceptual experiences" does not help me understand whether these are perceptual differences or affective differences.[104] Searle's identification of quale as "the qualitative aspect of our conscious experiences" skirts the very issue it should address—is this qualitative effect sensory-perceptual, or is it affective (an overtone of consciousness)?[105] Elsewhere discussing "subjective feelings" (aren't all feelings subjective?) he states, "The essential thing about pain is that it is a specific, internal, qualitative feeling."[106] This equates pain and its quality. Is it not really that pain *has* a quality? (More about this later when we discuss the two pain systems.) More helpful is the contrast with quanta so that qualia relate to quality as quanta relate to quantity. But then, to muddle this suggestion, the examples of qualia given in the *Oxford Companion to the Mind* are the smell of coffee or the taste of pineapple, experiences that "have a distinctive phenomenological character which we have all experienced, but which, it seems, is very difficult to describe"—experiences that are sensory and that have a quality. Why not accept the *OED* definition of quale as "the quality of a thing" in a sense independent of the sensation with which it is associated? Pineapple is sweet, tart, and wet (sensations) and tastes pineappley (a quale).

If the suggestion of two systems operating in parallel has any value, then the notion that "qualia are high-order discriminations that constitute consciousness" can be only partially correct.[107] That is so because, according to this formulation, the feeling, tone, or emotional coloring called qualia is generated by the limbic system and cannot constitute high-order discriminations—unless, as he suggests elsewhere, Edelman means simply that a quale "is a subjective conscious state."[108] But, as Humphrey says (remembering that his use of the term *sensation*—implying affective—is different from the stimulus hierarchy proposed here), "The weight of evidence really does suggest that sensation and perception, although they are triggered by the same event, are essentially independent takes on this event, occurring not in series, but in parallel."[109]

The criterion of discrimination shifts the emphasis from feeling in the emotional sense to feeling in the somatosensory sphere when discrimination between refined differences of hot and cold is discussed. "It is in fact the ability to discriminate refined difference of, say, hot and cold in the presence of myriad other qualities such as color in a unitary scene that distinguishes a conscious discrimination from the hot-cold distinctions made, for example, by a thermostat."[110] No question about it. But sensory or perceptual experiences are not consciousness. They require consciousness in order to be experienced, and they are part of the consciousness–awareness duet; but they by themselves are not consciousness. Discrimination between fine differences in heat and cold is a matter of thermal degrees—a quantity, not a quality. This argument may not please John Searle, who writes, "The distinction between quantity and quality, by the way, is probably bogus. There is no metaphysical reason why you could not have measurements of the degree of pain or conscious awareness for example."[111] Well—yes and no. Yes to the second sentence, but no to the first. They really are not related. Certainly pain, and perhaps consciousness, have degrees. Awareness has degrees. But that is different from measured degrees of temperature, because we have a measuring system for temperature. And the degrees measured are in the stimulus object; they are not subjective, not degrees of hotness. Quantification of other stimuli has been accomplished (Frey hairs for pressure, as an example), but not for pain. Pain is a sensation that accompanies extremes of any sensory stimulus (hot, cold, pressure, sound), which is part of the reason pain has not been objectively quantified. Pain is not an attribute of the object (unlike, say, green). Conscious awareness, too, relates to multiple stimuli, making quantification far from systematic.

However, the measured degrees of the object are distinct from its subjective quality. Just as the greenness differs from the green, so the hotness differs from the hot. (And Humphrey's notion of redding, although it emphasizes action, does not really help).[112] Despite the Weber Fechner Law and the Stevens Power Law, "There is no way to measure sensation that is distinct from the measurement of the physical stimulus."[113] This could be viewed as a summary statement of the qualia problem. The subjective quale cannot be measured. The objective–subjective relationship expressed by the luminance–brightness pair must usually be classified by the unsatisfactory green–greenness or hot–hotness ratio. Pain, it turns out, has quality, and the amount of pain is distinct from its quality. Again, Searle might not agree. He writes "The problem of qualia is not just an aspect of the problem of consciousness, it *is* the problem of consciousness" (original italics).[114] But he goes on, "To the extent you are talking about conscious *discrimination* you are talking about qualia" (italics added).[115] Years ago, Henry Head distinguished between two types of pain: epicritic and protopathic. This is a qualitative distinction most of us can confirm—despite the initial criticism the idea elicited. Contrast what you feel when you prick a finger (epicritic) with abdominal cramps or a blow to the testes (protopathic).

Epicritic is sharp, fast, and well localized; protopathic is slower, diffuse, often crescendos, and (most important) has a different affective accompaniment—sickening, threatening. I do not mean to be technical (or contentious), but Searle's focus on C fibers in this context raises the point that this is only part of the pain delivery system. There is a second pathway that may account for pain of two qualities. Delta A fibers also participate. You can demonstrate this for yourself. In a quiet, contemplative situation, gently stick yourself with a pin—the proximal knuckle of the fourth finger turns out to be a good place. You will feel a bright, well-localized immediate pain, and shortly afterward a more diffuse, spreading, echo pain. Try it. If Searle's "qualitative feel" that is a quale can be construed as a quality, and the *OED* defines quale as "the quality of a thing," then Edelman's suggestion "that all conscious experiences are qualia" might be better stated "that all conscious experiences have qualities," a statement that allows the disjunction of the percept and its quality.[116] But Edelman, if I understand him, views it differently, for he says about the thalamocortical system, which he calls the dynamic core, "the activity of the core enables conscious animals to carry out high-order discriminations. Qualia *are* those discriminations" (original italics).[117] But these discriminations seem to be based on perceptual (rather than emotional) systems. "We already have ample evidence from neuroscience to suggest why different qualia have different *feels*. The neural structures and dynamics underlying vision are different from those of smell, as those for touch differ from those for hearing . . ." (italics added).[118] Yet, in his table of "Features of Conscious States" under the heading of "Subjective," he enters "1—They reflect subjective feelings, qualia, phenomenality, mood, pleasure and unpleasure": all reflections of a nonperceptual system. Putting qualia under subjective (feelings, mood, pleasure and "unpleasure") I understand to mean (to stay with Edelman's example) that the green of an object (the wavelength) contributes to the percept; the greenness of the object (really of the green) is contributed by the percipient. The confusion results from the use of "greenness" to indicate both the physical aspects—hue, saturation—and the psychophysical aspects—the quality and associated feeling tone. We speak of sad colors (I have the blues) in relation to affective psychophysical aspects, not wavelength, saturation, or hue. The affective aspects of color are discussed by Humphrey, who showed that Rhesus monkeys "have strong and consistent emotional responses to colored lights."[119] Humans, too, demonstrate emotional responses to colored lights, and "this is true even in babies as young as 15 days," emphasizing again the role of the limbic system (which is mature in infants). The implication of a limbic contribution is strengthened by Edelman's inclusion of "3—They give rise to feelings of familiarity or its lack." As Yogi Berra is alleged to have said, "Déjà vu all over again."

The counterpoise to a discussion of qualia is intentionality. If qualia are construed as subjective, intentionality might be thought to be objective, for it requires an object; but the object (real or conceived) is mentally represented. That representation is about the real or imagined world and is subjective. The term *intention* appears in discussions of consciousness and is defined as "abstract early plans for movements."[120] But these abstract early plans are distinct from motor programs, as is evident in movement disorders (tremor, athetosis, chorea, hemiballism) in which motor programs released by lesions are without intent, although there is awareness—that is, "consciousness of." Intentional action, to Freeman, is a component of intentionality, which he defines as having the properties of "intent or directness toward some future state or goal, its unity and its wholeness."[121] Unity and intent, he notes, find expression as *aboutness*. Thus, intentionality, a property of consciousness, is its aboutness. Those of us who are not philosophers cannot help but wonder about intentionality's relation to awareness; just as awareness must be of something, so aboutness must be about something. Searle says, "'Intentionality' is a technical term used by philosophers to refer to that capacity of the mind by which mental states refer to, or are about, or are of objects and states of affairs in the world other than themselves."[122] Banks, too, emphasizes the mental aspect by describing intentionality as "the mental state that leads to taking an action in relation to an object."[123] Dennett puts it more directly. "Intentionality in the philosophic sense is just aboutness."[124] This aboutness I understand to be perceptual or conceptual, but not emotional (contra Searle)—not a feeling or quale. The perceptual aspect is emphasized by Edelman when he writes about intentionality: "It is the property by which consciousness is directed at, or is about, objects and states of affairs that are *initially in the world*" (italics added).[125] These objects and states of affairs in the world serve as initial input to generate percepts, which in turn can generate concepts. Edelman emphasizes this later on the same page when speaking of the "initial development of conscious states." He says, "Insofar as this fundamental aspect of higher brain function depends on input from the world and the brain through various *modalities*, it is not surprising that in both conscious perceptual, and memorial states, intentionality is a central property" (italics added).[126] Recalling that perception and memory may exist as conjoined states, the implication is that intentionality is a manifestation of the specific pathway function—a possibility emphasized in the suggestion of input through "various modalities." In contrast, "not all conscious states (mood for example) are intentional."[127]

Searle distinguishes mood from emotional by the intentional aspect of emotion, an important philosophic point, but not included in the use of the word *emotion* here.[128] Here emotion is used to suggest an affective quality generated by limbic structures. A given emotion may be intentional. The term *emotion* need not be. Mood is a state of feeling—a quale generated by a nonperceptual neural system. This in contrast to Dennett, for whom "perceptual states, emotional states, and states of memory, for example, all exhibit aboutness."[129] How do we understand this in light of his remark, "Something exhibits intentionality if its competence is in some way *about* something else" (original italics)?[130] Is it that the emotional state (in the sense of affective state) lacks "aboutness" in itself and depends for its legitimacy on the percept or memory that it is about? Competence is the operative—though ambiguous—word. If the aboutness relates to the percept or memory to which it is attached, then consider it as a limbic-generated quale attached to a supralimbic function. Of course, emotional states can have intentionality as a referent when they are referred to—a conceptual function—but that is rather different from the affective state itself. Perhaps the easiest way to deal with intentionality is to give it up—deny its role in consciousness (or at least some forms of consciousness). Honderich says: "Our principle conclusion in this paper, then, is that we need to give up on propositions of intentionality . . . in connection with perceptual consciousness."[131]

To postulate a parcellation of qualia and intentionality into limbic and supralimbic substrates does not require a reformulation of the proposed neurological base on which consciousness is built. Humphrey states it this way: "While the old channel continues to provide an affect-laden, modality-specific, body-centered picture of what the stimulation is doing to the animal's own self, the second is set up to provide a more neutral, abstract, body-independent representation of the outside world."[132] Both limbic and supralimbic systems participate in conscious awareness. The thalamocortical assemblies (the dynamic core of Edelman) are active in both systems. The difference is that the specific thalamic nuclei and cortical primary projection areas that form the initial phase of the perceptual system do not participate in thalamic limbic projections. The thalamic contribution to the limbic assemblies—particularly by the anterior and dorsomedial nuclear groups—are not specific in the sense that they do not transmit modality-marked sensations; nor are they nonspecific in the sense of the intralaminar nuclei that receive non-modality-marked input from below and project widely. These early-formed limbic assemblies deal with prelinguistic ineffable feelings that are assigned intentionality through the medium of language and metaphor, by which they are expressed, or what Humphrey terms the "propositional paraphrase." As Chalmers says, "Our *language* for phenomenal qualities is derivative on our nonphenomenal language" (original italics).[133] It must be noted, however, that the states, not the linguistic representation of them, are assigned intentionality. Pain and mood, representative of consciousness without intentionality, now become intentional as Honderich indicates, although I don't think he approves.[134]

Limbic participation in the genesis of emotion or of mood, affect, and feelings is more than just by the thalamocortical and corticothalamic assemblies. Projections from the limbic cortex influence autonomic function. Heart rate, blood pressure, pupil size, respiration, and other autonomic activities can be modified by insular, orbitofrontal, and cingulate area input. Such autonomic activity often participates in emotional behavior—and in the James-Lange theory of emotion it is considered to *be* emotion. Autonomic activity has no aboutness, no intentionality, because the organism usually is not consciously aware of it. This now old-fashioned theory (James published in 1884, Lange in 1885) speaks directly to objections such as those raised by Harnad, who asks how the feeling is generated—rather than what its correlates are. James-Lange addresses that question by moving the feeling or emotion from the autonomic-limbic to the somatosensory and stating that the feeling of *bodily changes* as they occur *is* the emotion. This really does not solve the issue of how the feeling is generated, but it introduces two interesting consequences: (1) the notion of feedback; bodily changes, mostly autonomic, are fed back by way of (2) a somatic (rather than an autonomic) sensory system, and they come to the awareness of which autonomic function is usually deprived—or, as Luria puts it, "delegation from a proprioceptive origin to an exteroreceptive surrogate permits increased conscious regulation of behavior."[135] The "self-monitoring of the subject by his own response is the prototype of 'feeling sensation' as we humans know it."[136]

Extending the James-Lange approach to consciousness allows us to put the argument in its strongest form. The problem is a conceptual one. It is a perpetuation (to my unphilosophical mind) of the remnants of dualism. This dualism is reflected in the separation of correlates and consciousness, of feelings and self; for it creates an explanatory gap and requires bridge principles. "There is an *explanatory gap* between the physical level and conscious experience," says Chalmers (italics in the original).[137] "A physical theory gives a theory of physical processes, and a psychophysical theory tells us how these processes give rise to experience. . . . I call it *naturalistic dualism*" (italics in the original).[138] Naturalistic because "we can *explain* consciousness in terms of basic natural laws" (original italics).[139] But he goes on to say that "this dualism could turn out to be a kind of monism. Perhaps the physical and the phenomenal will turn out to be two different aspects of a single, encompassing kind, in something like the way that matter and energy turn out to be two aspects of a single kind."[140] In the James-Lange type of model, neural activity is not a correlate of consciousness; it is not even causative of consciousness. Neural activity is consciousness just as neural activity is the feeling (emotional or somatic) and not the correlate or cause of the feeling. And neural activity that is consciousness and that is feeling (separate neural activities) is not appreciated by a separate entity called the self. Consciousness and feeling are the self, their neural substrate (activity) is the self. If this seems far-fetched, recall that nowadays a quadriplegic can operate a computer just by thinking. The neural activity "represents" the activity on the computer. Perhaps the most recent statement of this view is "consciousness is an attribute of network activity and has no independent existence. Consciousness has no causal powers over and above the causal powers of the corresponding neural activity. Therefore whatever one (i.e. the brain) does consciously or intentionally is done by the underlying mental/neural operations rather than by being conscious per se."[141] Clearly this formulation cannot be tested by the usual scientific method, but lack of scientific verifiability or falsification should not by itself vitiate the conceptual value. Neither should the invective that claims the problem has been solved by denying its existence, which is, after all, only the obverse of creating problems that do not exist. This does not solve the binding problem. It does not explain how the components of a system cohere to form a whole. It does not explain how systems are bound together to allow cross-modal experience. It does not explain how experience is attached to consciousness or how consciousness can be attached to memory of the past or prediction of the future. But it gets rid of that first gap between the objective and the subjective, between the physical and the psychophysical. In one sense the binding problem is the problem of representation—that is, how a percept (say) composed of many features can be represented in the brain as a coherent whole—as an entity, or a unity. This is of more than passing interest in any discussion of consciousness (which is generally conceived to be unified), because the unity of consciousness may be a specific instantiation of a generalized mechanism responding to (described by) the same principles that apply to sensory (broad sense) and motor systems.

Discussions of consciousness often cite the unity of consciousness as a defining feature. What is never clear is whether the unity applies to the percept (its individual components bound together into a unity, where percept is taken to refer to an object and its ambient environment) or to the underlying sentient state on which the percept is displayed. Edelman writes "One outstanding property is that consciousness is unitary or integrated" but later writes that "This unitary scene will change and differentiate according to outside stimuli . . ."[142] The first part of the sentence implies a background state, the second part a perceptual foreground. Similarly, Libet speaks of the "unitary nature of thought or conscious *experience*" (italics added), suggesting a unified percept or concept.[143] Searle indicates that unity applies to the state of consciousness when he speaks of "unified conscious fields" not divisible in the way physical objects—and therefore their percepts—are.

The issue is whether we are talking about the binding of sensory input to form a unified perceptual experience or whether consciousness—perhaps a coalescence (binding) of the output of several assemblies—is a separate process. If the latter is the case (as I believe), then consciousness—the state—may be sustained by a comparatively small number of interchangeable modular assemblies independent of perceptual accompaniments and can be viewed as operating in parallel with the perception with or without awareness of it.

Representation figures in many theories of neurologic organization from Hughlings-Jackson's representation, re-representation, and re-re-representation to Domasio's first-order maps projecting to second-order maps to the hierarchy of afferent-sensory-perceptual-conceptual that I like to employ. How does this representation and re-representation come about? Clearly we still don't know, but a great deal of recent work (summarized by Singer in Metzinger) explores this area. Singer distinguishes two strategies employed by the brain to represent contents. One consists of single neurons tuned to particular input activity to "establish explicit representation of particular constellations of features."[144] I suppose the grandmother cell belongs here. The second strategy employs assemblies— "A temporary association of neurons into a functionally coherent 'whole.'"[145] The important question of what produces the temporary anatomically widely dispersed assemblies may be answered by the synchronization of response. This synchronization results in the gamma frequency oscillation that has been demonstrated in the olfactory, visual, auditory, somatosensory, and motor systems. Synchronization is facilitated or enhanced when the cortical EEG is desynchronized—an effect of the mesencephalic ascending reticular activating system activity. "Brain states that are compatible with the manifestation of consciousness also favor the emergence of ordered spatiotemporal activity patterns which could serve as the substrate for the formation of assemblies."[146] Because Singer's hypothesis is important, his five assumptions should be quoted. "(1) Phenomenal awareness necessitates and emerges from the formation of metarepresentations; (2) The latter are realized by the addition of cortical areas of higher order that process the output of lower-order areas in the same way as the latter processes their respective input; (3) In order to account for the required combinatorial flexibility, these metarepresentations are implemented by the dynamic association of distributed neurons into functionally coherent assemblies rather than by individual specialized cells; (4) The binding mechanism that groups neurons into assemblies and labels their responses as related is the transient synchronization of discharges with a precision in the millisecond range; (5) The formation of such dynamically associated, synchronized cell assemblies requires activated brain sites characterized by 'desynchronized' EEG and is facilitated by attentional mechanisms."[147]

Because this is important, it warrants restatement. Low gamma-frequency oscillations (brain waves in the range of 30–70 Hz) have been implicated in the genesis of consciousness. These oscillations are generated in the thalamus and cortex and are synchronized in corticothalamic networks. They appear in the waking state and during REM sleep and relate to attention focused on internal or external stimuli. Endogenous REM stimuli and exogenous sensory stimuli evoke the same type of gamma frequency response. The evocation by sensory stimuli suggests a relation between gamma oscillations and awareness as distinct from (intransitive) consciousness. Binding, which is customarily related to awareness of percepts, has been attributed to oscillations in the gamma range because coherent oscillations have been observed over widely separated areas of cortex. Koch and Crick (for whom awareness is synonymous with consciousness) suggest that "awareness is associated with phase locked oscillatory firing behavior in the 35–65 Hz frequency range."[148] The notion that synchronized activity, such as that in the gamma frequency band, produces transient formation of cell assemblies may be correct but does not allow for distinction between assemblies which underlie percepts (and their awareness) and those that underlie consciousness. However, the thalamocortical loop is a prominent candidate for the genesis of consciousness with the number of feedback pathways from the cortex an order of magnitude higher than that of thalamocortical projections. Its candidacy is championed by the participation of the thalamic intralaminar nuclei, which can generate rhythmic

bursts in the gamma range and which project widely to cortex. In this formulation, binding of various attributes of a percept is imposed by the
phase-locked gamma frequency generated—at least in part—by the
"consciousness mechanism" of the thalamic intralaminar nuclei. Of
interest concerning the role of the ascending reticular activating system
in the consciousness "state" is its ability to enhance gamma frequency
oscillation in cortical sensory, motor, and attention areas.

Honderich, writing for philosophers (Searle, Humphrey and Dennett
are writing for the rest of us), is difficult to translate. The risk of category
confusion is great. For example Searle, writing about the unity of consciousness, writes of the subjective. Honderich, writing about the unity of
consciousness, writes about the subject. The two are quite distinct: The
subjective state of consciousness "is by its very essence qualitative, subjective and unified."[149] The "subject is one thing, consciousness itself,
rather than four things. Our subject is not consciousness + the purely
neural or brain facts that go with consciousness + the causes of consciousness + the effects of consciousness. But there is certainly a ten-
dency in much current philosophy of mind to think that this large bundle
is the subject of consciousness."[150]

Honderich's reference to the philosophy of mind, Searle's book *Mind*,
Chalmers's *The Conscious Mind*, and Dennett's *Kinds of Minds* emphasize
the philosophical coalescence of the connection between consciousness
and mind. To me they are quite distinct. Consciousness, in its most fundamental physiological form, is necessary for mind—but not the other
way around. Only in its more elaborated cerebral manifestation is the
conflation of consciousness with mind justified. It is only at the cerebral
level that the "*idea* of a subject of self, or maybe just awareness" (italics
added)—what I would construe as self-consciousness—can be generated.[151] And, once again, this results from the equation of consciousness
with awareness, a customarily joined pair that should nevertheless be
separated. So, when Honderich writes, "It seems contents do not merely
occur on their own," I understand this to be the conscious awareness of
contents that "seem to occur for or to a subject," which I understand to
be a conscious self.[152] But when he says, "Nor do we suppose there are
bare subjects without contents, awareness of *nothing*" (original italics),
the crucial word is awareness, which should not be construed as consciousness.[153] Indeed, he goes on to suggest, by indirection, an accept-
ance of the low level or readiness form of consciousness generated in the
brain stem when he writes: "It is fairly widely accepted that there are law-
like connections between the neural and that part of consciousness that
seems *not* to fall under the intentional characterization" (original ital-

ics).[154] This is as much of a surprise as when Searle, for whom consciousness is a unity, writes: "Consciousness is not spread out like jam on a piece of bread, but rather it comes in discrete units."[155] I believe this to be true at the cortical level, where the unified entity, like a mosaic, is made up of many small interchangeable parts, the interchange of which does not alter the larger picture. One analogy—which should not be taken literally—posits a bright figure against a less bright ground. The brightness is determined by location and is not an inherent attribute of the exchangeable part—in the way that the voltage applied at a given location determines the brightness of the replaceable, exchangeable lightbulb. Thus, the percept shines against the background cortical consciousness, which, while nonspecific, nonetheless serves as context because it simultaneously provides a specific display. This helps understand how to formulate a possible answer to Honderich's question: "If the same piece of language means different things in different linguistic settings, but goes with exactly the same type of neural event, no doubt complex and ramified, how can the facts of consciousness be taken to depend on just that neural event?"[156] The piece of language is composed of high-voltage bright bulbs, the different linguistic setting (the ground or environment of the action) the low-voltage background glow. Both contribute to awareness because both are mediated by the specific systems, while both contribute to consciousness because the modules (interchangeable parts) also receive input from the nonspecific system. The same piece of language in a different linguistic setting does not—cannot—go with exactly the same type of neural event. The neural substrate of the background must be different, and even the neural correlate of the foreground may be different. The high-voltage bulb—to return to the analogy—may not always receive the same voltage.

Honderich discusses Searle's thirteen truths about consciousness. He finds that: 1) Conscious events are physical events. 2) Conscious events are brain events. 3) Conscious events are subjective. 4) Consciousness is unitary. 5) Conscious events correlate with the five types of modalities related to the five senses. 6) Conscious events evolve a figure-ground relationship. They also involve: 7) Pervasive familiarity; 8) Overflow, or the connection of thoughts with other thoughts; 9) Selective attention; 10) Boundary conditions; 11) Mood; 12) A pleasure–unpleasure dimension; and 13) Intentionality. "None of the thirteen features of consciousness gives us the needed conception";[157] "nor is light shed by a bluff confidence in humble truths."[158]

Hobson, too, has thirteen simple truths about consciousness—he calls them building blocks: 1) Sensation; 2) Perception; 3) Attention; 4) Emotion;

5) Instinct; 6) Memory; 7) Thought; 8) Language; 9) Intention (meaning representation of goals); 10) Orientation; 11) Learning; 12) Volition; and 13) Movement. But this is no help—particularly when he refers to 1–5, 11, and 13 as "mostly unconscious and automatic."[159]

Honderich gives me great pleasure by his discussion of "Seeing Things." He starts by identifying "perceptual consciousness"—or conscious awareness, in our terms. He identifies "what seems to be fundamental to consciousness, which is perceptual consciousness—our being aware of things around us by sight and our other senses. There can be little doubt that perceptual consciousness not only preceded other consciousness in the development of our species, but also is prior in other ways, say in the early development of a human being, however complex that story."[160] He doesn't say it came first: he doesn't say it is rudimentary: he doesn't say it didn't grow out of something else. He simply says it has two components, only one of which is perceptual (that of which we are aware). And of course percepts always differ one from another. The other component, which is harder to define, permeates all perceptual consciousness and is unitary, featureless, and more or less the same in all mental events. The content rides on it "like the idea of a passenger."[161] How nicely this fits with the nonspecific brain stem projection to the cortex, unmarked by modality, widely distributed, always present, and everywhere (in cortex) the same, carrying the percept as a passenger. "The different and many-featured property of each of most of our visual experiences *is* its content. As for the property that is more or less the same in each of our otherwise different visual experiences and is unitary, this can be referred to as its *subject*. In my view all mental events can be spoken of with some reason as a matter of subject and content. That is what mental events are. The nature of the mental, of consciousness, consists in this internal duality" (original italics).[162] I understand him to use subject in the sense of self—not in the sense of topic, or what it is about (introducing confusion, the subject—i.e., the what it is about—of visual experiences being its intentionality). Earlier he has said that "our idea of consciousness is the idea of a subject or self, or maybe just awareness."[163] I wish he had said "consciousness" instead of "subject," in which setting content becomes perceptual awareness. But he goes on to make it even more difficult. "The term 'subject' is very rightly suspect . . . My use of 'subject' is not to be taken as conveying more than what has already been mentioned. A subject is not a self unless a self is taken to be no more than a uniform part of a mental event which is like a part of other mental events which typically are otherwise different."[164] Oh dear!

Another problem for me—because I consider the negative or absence of a function (as seen in pathological dissolution of neurological function) as offering access to the absent function is his claim: "If there are ways or techniques of bringing things into consciousness, perhaps dispositions of ours of which we have been unaware, these are not a different access to consciousness itself. As for those very dispositions, often called the subconscious or the unconscious, evidently they are not *in* or part of consciousness. No doubt they are neural. To repeat what we don't have isn't consciousness, and we don't *have* it in more ways than one" (original italics).[165] I suppose this to be subconscious or unconscious in the psychiatric sense, not subliminal in the perceptual or agnosic in the pathologic sense. Even so, does this not conflate awareness with consciousness?—and does this not offer a potential route for examination of the separability of consciousness and awareness?

Discussion of this subconscious or unconscious allows a transition to psychiatric states. Both Honderich and Edelman refer (in both cases in passing, so I must not make too much of it) to hallucinations: the former in relation to perception, the latter in relation to consciousness. Honderich notes, "in perception we cannot be aware of physical objects, since hallucination where there are no such objects is indistinguishable from perception."[166] In fairness this is not a view he supports for later he states "the objection from hallucination needs to be regarded as what it is, advocacy of an impossible theory."[167] Still he talks about it again.[168] Edelman writes: "And, of course, there may be diseases of consciousness, such as schizophrenia, in which hallucinations, delusions and disorientation can occur."[169] Leaving aside "disorientation" (are schizophrenics disoriented?—it is "a state of mental confusion as to time, place or identity," according to Dorland's *Medical Dictionary*), these two citations demand a discussion of hallucinations, however eccentric it may be. Hallucinations are generally agreed to be percepts in the absence of external stimuli. If we are to accept the separation of conscious perception into consciousness and perception, then Edelman's suggestion of a "disease of consciousness" might be more accurately phrased "a disease of perception." Honderich accepts hallucinations as perception in the absence of external stimuli but does not (since it is not essential to his main thesis) explore the perceptual structure of the hallucination. Pertinent to this exploration is a separation of hallucination from illusion in the psychiatric sense of the term—a false interpretation of a real sensory image (Dorland). Hallucinations characteristically occur in one of three conditions: 1) Toxic or metabolic disorders including delirium; 2) Psychiatric states such as schizophrenia; 3) Stimulation of cerebral cortex at surgery or by seizures. How carefully do we evaluate the structure of the hallucination when it occurs? How certain are we that it exists? I have never been able to convince myself of the fully formed nature of the hallucinatory percept. I have never been able to convince myself (heresy of heresies) of the existence of hallucination in the strict sense of the term. In toxic or metabolic encephalopathy the hallucination turns out to be (in the psychiatric sense) an illusion. In schizophrenia it may be an illusion or it may be a dissociated affective state similar to the dissociated sensory state of the hallucination of cerebral stimulation. Not to pursue this too far (more in note 170 if you are interested)—in the schizophrenic the hallucinations are usually "voices." Many who appear to be hallucinating will not admit to hearing voices perhaps because of the way we phrase the question: "Are you hearing voices?" Shouldn't we ask, "Are you hearing something?" Perhaps what they hear is not voices. It is the operation of the nervous system on whatever it is that is heard that turns it into voices. When asked what the voices are saying, the patient who will admit to hearing voices will reply something like, "bad things." This is not an answer to the question "What are the voices saying?" so the question is repeated. A typical second reply would be, "They are calling me names." Again this is not an answer to the question—this is an interpretation of what I suspect is an ill-formed percept, an affective state or an illusion.

Is there any agreement in all that precedes? Is there any place where ideas and theories coalesce or at least intersect? Unity of consciousness might be the best candidate, for both physical scientist and philosopher acknowledge it. To Edelman, "one outstanding property is that consciousness is unitary."[171] To Koch, who may have an idiosyncratic definition—but for whom it exists—it is that, "in the presence of ambiguity, the mind doesn't supply multiple solutions but prefers a single interpretation that may change with time. This aspect of experience is sometimes referred to as the *unity of consciousness*" (original italics).[172] For Searle, too, consciousness is unified; he talks of it in an interesting way. Having previously thought of its three features—qualitativeness, subjectivity, and unity—he now thinks of them as aspects of the same phenomenon. "Consciousness is not divisible in the way that physical objects typically are; rather consciousness always comes in discrete units of unified conscious fields."[173] I understand these discrete units to be temporal rather than spatially interchangeable. This generally accepted unity is reconceived as a trinity by Honderich, who distinguishes perceptual consciousness (awareness by sight and other senses), reflective consciousness (thinking or conceptualization), and affective consciousness (desires, feelings, emotions, attitudes, and sensations). Perceptual consciousness "not only preceded other consciousness in the development of our species but is also prior in other ways, say in the early development of a human being."[174] All three, it seems to me, relate to the specific system-based aspect of consciousness and, although separate in developmental time, may in the mature evolved organism constitute a triune.

Can we get a consensus from all of this? It seems not, and perhaps it is just as well, for the problems of what consciousness is and of how (and where) it is formed—as well as other important aspects—remain. So it is well to have many views, many approaches, and even dispute. Dispute, however, implies a common ground—a common language. In these readings, the ground keeps shifting, and the language changing. What a word means for one writer may be quite different from its meaning for another. Indeed, even a single author will use a word in several (or in ambiguous) ways. "We have learned in recent philosophy of mind that the language of consciousness is easily degraded. The meanings of terms can be reduced to what is far less than the realities the terms are supposed to be about."[175] An early step in the required interdisciplinary approach should be the development of a common language—or, if separate languages are to be used, a dictionary that defines unambiguously the terms that are used so they can be understood by all.

But perhaps a consensus can be achieved if we look beyond the language to the implications—or at least to the inferences that may be drawn. Thus two important areas may each contain more agreement than is initially apparent. They are the questions of whether organizational principles that apply to other areas of neurologic function can be applied to consciousness, and whether consciousness and awareness are separable.

One of the principles of organization of the nervous system is recursion—the representation hierarchy of Hughlings-Jackson.[176] It is seen in individual systems, such as the motor system, as well as in the coalescence of systems to function as a totality. It appears in the organization of the consciousness "system," where it is given the special status of causative. It correlates with gamma oscillations, which in turn correlate with attention (consciousness), perceptual binding, and long-distance coordination of distinct brain areas. Edelman calls it "re-entry." Speaking of his dynamic core he says: "The core sends signals mainly to itself and its re-entrant interactions are assumed to give rise to conscious states."[177] Crick asks whether awareness, which to him is synonymous with consciousness, is the brain talking to itself. "In neural terms this might imply that re-entrant pathways . . . are essential."[178] Koch classifies this as "feedback" and says that conscious perception would not occur if feedback pathways from the front of the brain to the back were blocked."[179] All agree that recursion (called re-entry, feedback, loops, and reverberant circuits) is part of the conscious-producing mechanism. Most imply that it is unique to consciousness. I suggest that, just as the unity of consciousness is not unique but is a manifestation of the binding process seen in other systems, so re-entry to generate consciousness is a manifestation of the recursion that operates in other subsystems that combine to form the nervous system.

A second major issue to be addressed is the separability of consciousness and awareness. Here it seems to me that both the physical scientists and the philosophers—all of whom show reluctance to deal with this—accept it by implication. Among the physical scientists, Koch is the most explicit. He deals with the brain stem ascending reticular activating system (in the broad sense) head-on. He calls it an enabler of the NCC, but agrees that 1) it is neural and 2) it is not a content provider (almost there). Edelman redefines this as ascending systems that he calls value systems, which include many of the anatomic sites subsumed by the ascending reticular activating system (broad sense) such as locus coeruleus, raphe nucleus, hypothalamic nuclei, and others, which project diffusely to hemispheres and bias neuronal response (not quite there). Crick is the most tentative. Reticular formation controls general arousal and various stages of sleep. Signals go to neocortex and are widely distributed—but closer than that he won't come. And, to Hobson, "the reticular formation emerges as the coordinator, internal communicator and unifier of activity in the modular brain," but "consciousness is awareness."[180] It is Flohr who gives the strongest argument and offers a mechanism of action. The brain stem ascending reticular activating system adjusts the resting potential of the membranes in which the NMDA receptors are imbedded to bring it closer to threshold to prime cortex and prepare it to respond.

The philosophers address this by way of intentionality. Seen from a great distance by a non-philosopher (tread lightly) the subject of intentionality speaks directly—and in the affirmative—to the question of whether consciousness and awareness are distinct. That intentionality is aboutness, that aboutness has an object (is about something) and that most consciousness has intentionality all seem to indicate a distinction between the consciousness and the object of its aboutness. This is put in sharp relief when, as both Searle and Honderich tell us, consciousness is demonstrated to exist without intentionality. If consciousness has an object (of awareness) and can also exist independent of its object, then consciousness and awareness are separable.

Some of the books on consciousness employ introspection as the analytic tool. One searches for the soul and the site of free will. Rarely is behavior of others in the clinical and non-clinical world discussed, an approach I find congenial and productive—and one that I will pursue as we move on.

How apposite is Alexander Pope when he writes:

"Know then thyself," (the philosopher's approach)
"Presume not God to scan" (the search for the soul)
"The proper study of Mankind" (both on the subway and in the clinic)
"is Man."[181]

4

Where It Begins:
Anatomy and Environment

Consciousness, however defined, is a manifestation of brain function. Accordingly it is appropriate to begin a discussion of consciousness with an overview of the organization of the nervous system.

For purposes of classification, the nervous system is divided into a central and a peripheral component. The latter, composed of nerves and plexuses, transmits between the environment and the central nervous system's brain and spinal cord.

The environment may be conceived of as consisting of three concentric spheres relating respectively to neural derivatives of the three concentric embryonic layers—the germinal, the mantle, and the marginal. The innermost, composed of the organism's viscera and related structures, transmits information by way of the autonomic nervous system— a collection of nerve cells and fibers that originate in the innermost layers of the central nervous system and do not require voluntary control. Information from this layer is transduced by receptors called interoceptors.

The second environmental layer (really a sphere) that is interposed between the viscera and the external world is the body wall, neurologically served by cells aggregated in deeply located nuclei in what may be viewed as a middle neurological layer. Information from this middle

Consciousness, however defined, is a manifestation of brain function.

environment is conveyed to the nervous system by way of receptors termed proprioceptors.

The most external environment—the outside world—is represented in the outmost layer of the central nervous system (particularly the cerebral cortex), which receives information collected by exteroceptors (sometimes called teloreceptors), such as the eye or ear.[1]

Information is transmitted from the three environments to the nervous system by way of nerve fibers (axons and dendrites), which are projections from nerve cells. Axons are ensheathed by fatty white myelin insulation. Aggregates of axons are called white matter. Nerve cell bodies are not myelinated and form gray matter, whether in discrete regions (called nuclei) or in layers (called cortex). The gray matter of the spinal cord is located deep inside and is surrounded by the white matter of nerve fibers. This is in contrast to the cerebral hemispheres, in which the folded outer cortex is made of gray nerve cell bodies, and the myelinated white matter lies deep.

Axons may course in bundles that, peripherally, form nerves. Centrally these bundles are called fillets, tracts, pathways, or lemnisci. Customarily they project to collections of nerve cell bodies which, by their axons, relay the information farther along. Fillets are usually modality-specific, conveying information about a single sensory function on the input side. The nuclei to which they project are also often modality-specific.

Fibers may project in a widely distributed fashion rather than in bundles, terminating in dispersed nerve cell bodies. They are spoken of as reticular fibers (because of the reticulate pattern they create) and terminate on reticular nuclei that are considerably less well circumscribed than the terminal nuclei of lemniscal systems. Reticular pathways are often modality-unspecific or unmarked—despite receiving collaterals from lemniscal systems.

The central nervous system is divided into brain and spinal cord. The brain is re-divided into a brain stem, subcortical nuclei (including diencephalon) and cortex. As the phylogenetic tree is ascended, the rostral (cephalad) components increase in size by a greater proportion than do the lower components. The exuberant growth of the cortical mantle causes a transition from the lissencephalic smooth brain of smaller mammals to a gyrencephalic cortex, which achieves maximum expression in humans. The advent of the hills and valleys of gyri and sulci allows a major increase in surface area of the cortex without a proportional increase in brain volume (which would require a corresponding enlargement of head size, with its associated problem of support).

The spinal cord—the oldest component of the central nervous system—communicates with the periphery (the three environments) by way of peripheral nerves. These bring information to the nerve cells of the spinal segments, from which responses are returned to the effectors (muscles and glands) at the periphery. Fibers may also be projected rostrally to the brain stem, cerebellum, and cerebral structures. The lowest-level behavior is produced in the spinal cord and consists of a monosynaptic reflex formed by an incoming impulse in a fiber that synapses on a cell whose axon conducts an outgoing impulse. The connection between nerves is called a synapse; when, as here, there is only one, this forms a monosynaptic reflex arc.

Information is conveyed in nerve fibers by trains of electrical impulses. Each impulse is called an action potential, or spike, and is propagated unchanged along the nerve fiber until the synapse, where, by various means that include the release of transmitter chemicals, and by electrical transmission across gap junctions, the next nerve cell is excited. That cell then propagates an impulse along its axon to the next level. Impulses approaching a nerve cell are called afferent; those leaving a nerve cell are spoken of as efferent. Clearly an efferent impulse with respect to the first cell in a chain is afferent with respect to the second. Chains of neurons and their processes conduct information from the periphery to various levels of the nervous system. Fibers in these chains may branch so that information conducted to one neural level may, by a collateral branch, arrive at another location as well.

The brain stem is the lowest part of the central nervous system situated in the skull. It is divided anatomically into the medulla, pons, and midbrain, proceeding rostrally from spinal cord. It can, however, be considered as a single entity, for all three components transmit the same fiber bundles and contain the nuclei of the cranial nerves. The cranial nerves—of which there are twelve pairs—connect, just as the spinal nerves do, with the periphery. These subsume the functions of structures in and around the head and supplement the autonomic functions of spinal cord. Hearing, taste, eye movement, swallowing, and movement of the face and tongue are all functions of the cranial nerves. Sights and smells mediated by cranial nerves do not pass through the brain stem but go directly to the cerebrum. Much of the specific input to the brain stem is projected rostrally to subcortical and cortical areas for each individual modality. In addition non-lemniscal systems terminate on nuclei in brainstem reticular formation from which thalamic or extrathalamic projections are distributed widely to cortex.

Astride the brainstem sits the cerebellum, which, like the cerebrum, has an outer cortex and deep-seated nuclei. It receives input from spinal cord, brain stem, and cerebral hemispheres, and it projects to thalamus and cerebrum.

Among the subcortical nuclei of cerebral hemispheres the diencephalic thalamus is of particular interest. It is a collection of nuclei, some of which receive modality-specific lemniscal input. These are called specific, or relay, nuclei. They send fibers to their respective cortical primary projection areas. Thus vision is relayed from the retina by the optic nerve and optic tract to the lateral geniculate body in the thalamus and then to the striate cortex, which is called the primary visual area. Similarly audition, via the thalamus, terminates in the primary acoustic cortex of the temporal lobe. Cutaneous and body wall sensations transmitted by spinal and brain stem lemnisci (posterior columns of the spinal cord and medial lemniscus of brain stem as a representative case) are relayed by thalamic ventral posterior nuclei to the somatosensory cortex in the parietal lobe.

The thalamus also contains nonspecific nuclei that are modality-nonspecific and project widely to cortex, terminating in specific and nonspecific regions. These nonspecific thalamic nuclei extend through the entire thalamus and appear in the internal laminae that separate other nuclei. Input to the nonspecific thalamic nuclei comes from the ascending brain stem reticular formation, which also passes to cortex by an extrathalamic route.

Other cerebral subcortical nuclei (caudate, putamen, globus pallidus, claustrum, and amygdala) are imbedded in the large collection of white subcortical fibers. These white bundles connect: 1) One hemisphere with another (usually to homologous areas) by way of the corpus callosum and anterior commissure; 2) Part of one hemisphere to another part of the same hemisphere by such means as the arcuate fasciculus, the fronto-occipital bundle, and U fibers; and 3) Part of one hemisphere to lower levels such as thalamus, brain stem, and spinal cord. Central nervous system fiber bundles are termed projection systems when they course between levels of the nervous system either homolaterally or contralaterally, commissural systems when they course contralaterally at the same level, and association systems when they course ipsilaterally at the same level.

Cerebral cortex has been divided into areas on an anatomical cellular architectonic basis, or on a physiological functional basis. Each hemisphere, (for there are two, separated by the large interhemispheric fissure and connected by the corpus callosum) can be divided front-to-back by the central rolandic sulcus. It is taught that cortex in front of the central sulcus is motor (that is efferent) and that cortex behind the central sulcus is sensory (afferent including vision and audition). This generalization works well for the disinterested student but is not strictly true and creates conceptual problems. Architectonically, some of the most typical sensory cortex is found in the motor area. Functionally, stimulation of sensory cortex may produce movement. Indeed the division of cortex into sensory and motor components is as unjustified as the separation of stimulus from response, for, strictly speaking, a stimulus is defined by a response. A physical event that does not evoke a response can only be considered as a physical event—not as a stimulus. So it is better to think of the input-output system of cortex as sensorimotor. The intimate relation of sensation and motor function is emphasized by the loss of motor activity of a limb that follows the cutting of all the dorsal roots that provide sensation to that limb.

Within each of the major lobes of the cerebral hemisphere are primary projection areas of cortex in which are represented primary functions such as vision, audition, somatic sensation, and motor activity. Adjacent these are second- and third-order regions in which the primary functions are modified or elaborated. These so-called association areas ultimately project to multimodal regions. As a working rule, it is true that each hemisphere deals with contralateral personal and extrapersonal space. The inner environment has no neurological laterality. In some of the "higher level" association areas, bilateral space may be represented. This has even been claimed for some primary projection areas.

It is not surprising that the late-evolving cerebral cortex should be concerned primarily with external space, but the internal environment is also dealt with. It is represented by older cortex located near the midline. First-order autonomic fibers arise in orbital, medial temporal, and insular cortex and convey autonomic impulses to the hypothalamus, the brain stem, and the spinal cord.

As the phylogenic scale is ascended, the cortical enrichment that occurs is caused largely by an increase in association areas. This presumably reflects evolutionary change. Lower mammals (so called macrosmats) have relatively small cerebral cortices in relation to their rhinencephalons, or smell brains. Humans (contrary to popular misconception) have a large rhinencephalon; proportionally, the later-developing cortex is considerably larger. The phylogenetically early-developing rhinencephalon, like the early-developing spinal cord, is characterized by white matter on its outside.

Concentric to the rhinencephalon is limbic cortex, also an early development (as indicated by its five cellular laminae—in contrast to the six layers of later-developing isocortex of primary projection and association areas). It is called limbic because of its relation to the foramen of Monro. In embryonic development the cerebral hemispheres appear on each side of the rostral neural tube as an outpouching of which the neck forms the foramen of Monro. With continued expansion it is as if the hemispheres grow forward, then up, then backward, then down, following the course of the letter C around the foramen of Monro. This puts limbic cortex immediately concentric to the rhinencephalon on the medial aspect of the hemisphere. The rhinencephalon and limbic cortex are ready to function at the start of extra-uterine life. Other systems (take vision as an example) may not mature for many months.

The limbic system, which is thought to be a substrate for emotion, functions before the acquisition of language. This prelinguistic system will continue to operate in parallel with later developing functions and, in adult life, may produce an affective accompaniment to perceptual or conceptual experiences. There is no language adequate to describe these episodes except for that of metaphor. Ineffable experiences of this type existed before brain development produced language to describe them, which may be why they are inexpressible. There is, for example, the well-known déjà vu phenomenon, in which an ordinary perceptual experience mediated by late-developing sensory cortex takes on an inappropriate intense affective feeling of familiarity (although the subject undergoing the experience often knows that the percept is not familiar). Usually this experience cannot be verbalized except for the perceptual content. Similar phenomena include sudden intense insights or revelatory experiences or, on the negative side of déjà vu, intense feelings of strangeness or unfamiliarity.[2]

I would suggest that conscious attention is operating in parallel with, and is not a manifestation of, the perceptual experience.

The parallel operation of more than one neurological system is a principle of neurological organization. It is generally taught that neural function is serial. The visual scene is experienced, transmitted to primary visual cortex, forwarded to association areas, and appreciated. This is true, but overlooks the many parallel operations occurring simultaneously. At the lowest level, these include the autonomic functions that control blood pressure, heart rate, respirations, and pupil size, all of which are a necessary background on which the perceptual experience is grafted—so too with proprioceptive and vestbibular function (middle layer of environment), which serve to make the experience possible. Limbic input gives the percept its affective cloak, and I would suggest that conscious attention is operating in parallel with, and is not a manifestation of, the perceptual experience.

5

Where It Began: Evolution

"The notion that 'mind' and 'consciousness' are attributes only of man, and that thought can be separated from instinct by naïve dichotomy, become[s] unthinkable when one grasps the sweep of evolutionary time. The slow continuity of the evolutionary process transcends even the great steps from mineral structure to sentience (biogenesis), and from organism to ego (psychogenesis). From the beginning of life to the beginning of self awareness and thought took some 1200 million years."[1]

If the three levels of consciousness have evolved as the nervous system has evolved, culminating in the correlation of self-consciousness with a fully developed forebrain, then a brief review of the evolutionary development of the central nervous system is appropriate. Fossil nervous systems do not now exist, so inferences can be drawn only from existing bony fossil containers. But a more expedient way is to assume that evolution is reflected in existing genera, drawing evolutionary conclusions from a comparison of currently available animals' central nervous systems; this is but a restatement of the doctrine of the irreversibility of evolution. It is true that the maturation of the developing human nervous system is also a rich source of inferences about the relation between evolving consciousness and the evolving nervous system; but the notion of phylogenetic recapitulation is not warranted, so it is best to look to existing phyla. "You can get some idea of the evolution of the brain—from fish through amphibia and reptiles, to mammals—by comparing the brains of animals living today."[2]

The outstanding evolutionary brain change, and the one that presumably correlates with the appearance of self-consciousness, is the exuberant growth of the prosencephalon (forebrain), called encephalization. Encephalization is defined as the evolutionary process that accounts for the increasing dominance of "higher" (meaning later) levels over the functional activity of "lower" regions.[3] This obviously implies a vertical organization of systems in which the later-derived phylogenetic levels modulate activity of the earlier-acquired (both phylogenetically and ontogenetically) levels. The horizontally stratified spinal cord, brain stem, and cerebral hemispheres—including subcortical nuclei and diencephalon—are integrated anatomically and functionally by the vertically organized systems typified by the sensory and motor pathways. These pathways are envisioned as consisting of reticular and lemniscal components.[4] The reticular, the earlier phylogenetic integrator of function, is a diffusely organized network of nerve cells and processes. On the input side it is represented by the ascending reticular activating system that underlies the first instantiation of consciousness and suggests that this level of consciousness is phylogenetically old. On the output side the reticular system deals with posture and basic stereotypical movements. The newer lemniscal system is more compact, more direct, and more specific in function. It is typified on the input side by the pathways that conduct specific sensations (pain, touch, vision, audition, etc.) and on the output side by the phylogenetically newer corticospinal tract, a compact, descending motor pathway concerned with skilled movement and with the functions of the distal extremities and digits—so, therefore, with the extra-personal space of the external environment. The projection of this so-called pyramidal tract to motor neurons in the spinal cord becomes increasingly more prominent as one ascends the primate phylogenetic tree. Prosimians, such as lemurs, have control of the whole hand, but not of separate digits—in contrast with monkeys and apes. Concomitant with the development of these motor and sensory systems is the elaboration of the autonomic and limbic systems, early phylogenetic acquisitions that evolved in parallel with the old cortex—the archicortex.

Phylogenetically, the cerebrum was initially based on the sense of smell. In primitive vertebrates it consisted of a pair of smooth outpouchings at the front of the brain. From these lobes projected bulbs serving olfactory functions. The cortex was restricted to archipallium, just as it is in existing amphibia. Neocortex relating to lemniscal systems had not yet evolved; manipulation of external space was limited but could occur, mediated by the early-developed limbic system. This manipulation implied intent (signaling a forthcoming action), a component of intentionality. The signaling of forthcoming action, much as the readiness potential, returns us to the problem of will, both in the sense of volition and in the sense of futurity. This component of intentional action does not require neocortex. It is supported by the archicortex of the ventral forebrain—the olfactory bulb, pyriform cortex, amygdala, striatal nuclei, and hippocampus, all early acquisitions antedating the advent of neocortex, suggesting that intentionality required only the presence of the limbic system. What is left unsaid in this formulation is whether goal-directed, so-called "reflex" behavior of lower forms in the absence of these anatomic structures implies intent.

In reptiles, a small new area, the neopallium, appeared on the surface. Early in history, divergence of the reptile forebrain occurred in two directions. One produced enlargement of the corpus striatum in the side walls of the forebrain, ultimately leading to the appearance of the avian brain. The second, in mammals, consisted of an enlargement of the upper part of the forebrain by an increase of cerebral cortex. At first this cortex was smooth—lissencephalic—but, with continued phylogenetic elaboration, it became convoluted. The gyri and sulci, or hills and valleys, allowed a disproportionate increase in ratio of surface to volume of the gyrencephalic brain of the fully evolved primate. The distinctive trait of the primate, in contrast to other mammals, is the development of a large brain (in proportion to body weight) the expansion of which "began earlier, proceeded more rapidly, and ultimately advanced much further" than in other groups of evolving mammals.[5] As the mammalian brain evolved, the boundaries of cortical areas became increasingly demarcated and structurally differentiated cytoarchitectonically.

In the archaic mammalian brain the large olfactory bulb projects well beyond the rostral border of the cerebral hemisphere. It projects from the part of hemisphere called the pyriform lobe—the olfactory cortex, or large "smell brain" of early mammals. The phylogenetically ancient cortex of pyriform lobe is known as the archipallium. Dorsal to the pyriform lobe and separated from it by the laterally located rhinal sulcus is a newer area termed the neopallium. This cortex, which is forecast in reptiles, is not present in submammalian vertebrates and is concerned with the reception of all sensory information except for smell. With progressive phylogenetic development the proportion of archicortex to neocortex declined and smell became subordinated to other sensory modalities—particularly vision—in more advanced creatures, such as primates in whom anterior placed eyes corresponded to an arboreal life.

The large olfactory bulbs are connected one to the other by way of the large anterior commissure connecting the two hemispheres. The corpus callosum, the major interhemispheric connection of primates, is absent in submammalian vertebrates and in mammals as advanced as marsupials, implying that the coordination of hemispheric function is limited. With an increase of neocortex, and of the importance of nonolfactory sensory input, the increase of size and importance of the corpus callosum occurs, as does an increase in the size and importance of the thalamus. The size of the thalamus, which projects to neocortex and receives sensory input from the lemniscal systems, increases—but neocortex develops in excess of its thalamic (therefore lemniscal) projections to create yet higher-order (poorly termed "association") areas. In primates, one hemisphere relates to the other, and the output of multiple cortical areas, perhaps involving more than one modality, coalesce. As the primate brain develops in phylogeny, a number of changes occur in external morphology. The rhinal sulcus and the pyriform lobe now appear medially, marking the great expansion of the neopallium. The lateral sulcus becomes more prominent as the temporal lobe develops. The visual cortical areas in the occipital lobe expand until the occipital brain occludes the cerebellum from view. The cerebellum has expanded its hemispheres—which have a reciprocal connection with cerebral neocortex—as the cerebral hemispheres have expanded. Cerebral sulci (most prominently the central sulcus) have developed as the gyrencephalic hemisphere has grown.

Finally, with phylogenetic evolution, comes histologic change. The neuropil, representing cellular connections, increases; it is estimated that the ratio of the volume of gray matter to the volume of its contained nerve cells is about 50 percent higher in humans than in chimpanzees. Primitive, five-layered limbic cortex is succeeded by six-layered isocortex—up to nine layers have been described. New cells appear, including the von Economo nerve cell (described in 1926), found only in the most evolved primates (humans and apes) and, perhaps, some whales. These unique cells occur in layer five of the anterior cingulate and fronto-insular regions—considered to be phylogenetically old, limbic transition zones to the neocortex—suggesting that, even as neocortex was evolving, so was older limbic cortex.

It is always dangerous to make the transition from structure to function on the basis of inference, although there is reason to believe not only in the presence of a relationship but also that structure and function may reflect each other. What conclusions, however tentative, can be drawn from an evolutionary (better called comparative) study of the brain concerning the appearance and type of consciousness that existed, or exists, in nonhuman animals?

First, the reticular substrate for the lowest level of consciousness was presumably present in animals as low on the scale as amphibia. This substrate provided the background state that allowed response to stimuli. The lemniscal system, also present in amphibia, transmit-

> *It is always dangerous to make the transition from structure to function on the basis of inference*

ted those stimuli and allowed for response. The response tokened the second stage of consciousness—awareness of the presence of a stimulus, but without the implication of awareness of the awareness. That, presumably, required a more elaborate cerebrum able to conceptualize. At what level that emerged must for now remain conjecture. What we know (from introspection) is that it is present in humans. Its mechanism is not known, but, if mirror neurons (which are thought to underlie empathy) participate, self-consciousness below humans may be present phylogenetically at least as low as the level of the old-world monkey, the argument being that empathy—"the imaginative projection of one's own consciousness into another" implies awareness of one's own consciousness.[6]

6

What Is It?:
Consciousness

One problem with any discussion of consciousness is defining the term—or even managing to describe the phenomenon. Part of this difficulty may be historical; take, for example, the Freudian notions of the unconscious and preconscious, or the medical term "semiconscious." Another part may relate to various disciplines that define it; for the consciousness of the psychologist is rather different from that of the philosopher. Perhaps most important is that consciousness is not a unitary phenomenon—or, more accurately put, is a composite entity. Often definitions have focused on one part to the exclusion of others. All too often the term is used in an ambiguous, ill-defined way. Distinction must be made between a conscious state—what I have termed a "readiness" or a potential to respond (but not in the sense of voltage, which, when coupled with the term readiness, refers to a different phenomenon)—and "conscious of" (an experience that is often perceptual). A further complication is that "conscious of" cannot be equated with awareness, for awareness can be conscious or can be unconscious (in the "of" sense— a distinction Libet makes as the "actual awareness" and the "detection" of a signal respectively, although these terms, when used, like "consciousness," in the lay sense, do little to clarify). The distinction between the transitive and intransitive terms is fundamental. Response to subliminal stimulation and normal actions based on procedural memory are representative of consciousness without awareness, as (I argue) are stages of deep sleep. To circumvent this dilemma, terms such as preconscious and cognitive unconscious have gained new prominence, and reference to pathologic states such as "blindsight" has become popular. Foreconscious is to be preferred to preconscious, which, as used by Freud, means capable of being brought into consciousness. If we are to use the term consciousness to mean awareness, why not use the term "conscious awareness" to distinguish it from unconscious awareness?

At the most elementary level, consciousness can be identified as a readiness on the part of the organism to receive and respond to stimuli at the cerebral level. Consciousness of this sort is not necessary for motor response, for at low levels spinal motor output can occur even in the absence of brain stem input. This attribute of readiness presumably is shared by all animals. It is not alertness, wakefulness, or arousal—for it is available to be called into service even when the organism is asleep, responding to stimuli from any of the three concentric environments. A full bladder, a painful muscle, or a loud noise each prove sufficient to cause full wakefulness. This readiness is generated in the brain stem reticular formation, which, like an idling motor, can "rev up" without significant latency. The electroencephalogram of sleep can convert abruptly to a waking electroencephalogram (although it must be noted that dissociation between the behavior pattern and the electroencephalogram pattern may exist in the presence of certain brain stem lesions). Only suppression of cortical function as profound as that produced by anesthesia causes true unconsciousness of "sleep." Anesthesia exercises its effects on the neuraxis in a descending sequence, suppressing cortex first. As the depth of anesthesia increases, lower levels are affected until ultimately all brain stem function can terminate.

Awareness is not a component of this level of consciousness any more than awareness is a component of certain neurological information inputs. These inputs, which can be termed afferent, do not reach consciousness awareness until they are disturbed. Representative of this class are postural inputs by the vestibular and proprioceptive systems. A hyperactive or deficient organ of equilibrium announces its presence unpleasantly; but when it functions properly, we are unaware of its existence. In the sense that "afferent" is neurological input of which the organism is unaware, the readiness level of consciousness can be construed as afferent. Brainstem impulses are received by cortex but do not reach awareness until attached to a percept. This input is widely dispersed in cortex, is devoid of sensory markers, is not lateralized with respect to external space, and does not require a fully developed or matured cerebrum to exist—as in the conscious newborn.

Disturbance of this readiness level of consciousness—in contrast with disturbance at other levels of consciousness—produces clinical unconsciousness, a state in which the organism does not respond to external, or even bodily, stimuli except at the lowest levels. As deduced from the mechanism of closed head injury, either of two processes may cause unconsciousness. One, the knockout blow, results in direct percussion of the brain stem. The momentum of the blow to the jaw is transmitted to the brain stem, which is propelled against the firm edge of the tentorium—the tough, unyielding dural membrane through which the brain stem passes. Percussion of the brain stem may interrupt a number of brain stem functions, including respiration, cardiac contraction, and brain stem reticular activating system output. A severe enough blow will cause death. That this type of unconsciousness results from the effects of the blow on the ascending reticular activating system and is not secondary to cardiovascular effects can be inferred from its immediate onset (anoxic or anemic effects would be delayed) and its occurrence without loss of cardiorespiratory function.

The second mechanism for loss of consciousness spares the brain stem and its reticular activating system and injures instead the region of termination of the reticular projection—the cerebral cortex. The usual cause is an acceleration/deceleration injury (an automobile accident, for example), in which the rapidly moving skull is suddenly stopped (as when it strikes the windshield). The momentum of the brain causes it to strike the skull, and it may bounce back and strike the skull again directly opposite the location of the initial impact—the so-called coup and contra coup injury. Impact paralyzes the cortical neurons and, if severe enough, causes loss of consciousness. The more severe the closed-head injury, the deeper and longer the state of unconsciousness. One indication that the site of injury is cortex is the permanent defect following recovery of consciousness, known as retrograde amnesia—memory generally considered to reside in the cerebral hemisphere. Retrograde amnesia is a loss of memory for events immediately preceding the impact. The more severe the depth and duration of unconsciousness, the longer the period of retrograde amnesia—that is, the longer before the impact the last memory took place, the more severe the injury.

Clinical loss of consciousness reveals information about the stimulus adequacy (Sherrington's term) of events in each of the three concentric environments as well as the response of each of the three concentric neurologic layers. Stimuli from the external environment are unable to activate the teloreceptors or their cortical projections. The patient is unaware of external events. Stimuli from the body wall may or may not be adequate to cause response. The unconscious patient may move—presumably because a noxious stimulus was appreciated. During loss of consciousness, stimuli from the inner body—the viscera—continue to evoke responses from the inner neural layer. Respiration, cardiac activity, blood pressure, digestion, and micturition usually continue uninterrupted during prolonged unconsciousness, even without conscious awareness. There is therefore a stimulus hierarchy having internal stimuli (often relating to the physical integrity of the organism) as the most biologically significant elements, requiring immediate response. Stimuli from the external world are the most facultative. This stimulus hierarchy is evident in other forms of neurological dissolution as well as in normal individuals.

> *The analog of focused attention with the consciousness system might best be called conscious awareness.*

Consciousness generated by afferent input without awareness of input is analogous to the attention system. Indeed, the relation between consciousness and the system that generates attention should be explored further, for it may be that the two—attention and consciousness—are but two manifestations of a single physiologic mechanism. The basic level of attention, like the fundamental level of consciousness, establishes a state of readiness to receive stimuli. This state of vigilance occurs, for example, when a subject is placed in a dark environment and told to report every flash of light that occurs. Brief flashes of light appear here and there, but the subject has no advance knowledge of where and when they will occur. The state of readiness that exists between flashes is called vigilance. Superimposed on vigilance is recognition or awareness of the flash (which is modality-marked). This is the result of focused attention. In Libet's formulation, awareness is akin to vigilance, for it is a unique phenomenon "associated with unique neuronal activities,"[1] is a common feature of all consciousness but differs from the content of awareness, and "content of an event can be determined by the brain unconsciously without awareness of it."[2] The desynchronized EEG of waking or REM sleep is not a sufficient indicator of the conscious state (or "readiness"), for the organism—and therefore the brain—is ready to respond (is in a conscious state) even during the depth of slow-wave sleep indicated by a synchronized or "inactive" EEG.

The analog of focused attention with the consciousness system might best be called conscious awareness. This implies sensory or perceptual input, for awareness cannot occur without awareness of something. The something must be a sensation or a percept. The terms sensory and perceptual are used here to indicate input that (unlike afferent) comes to awareness. They are afferent in terms of direction of input but imply higher neurological levels of processing. They differ one from the other in that sensory is unstructured or inchoate (for example pain, heat, or coldness). A percept, composed of multiple sensory inputs, is structured. Like sensory input, it requires the presence of a stimulus, but, unlike sensory input, it can be conceptualized in the absence of the external stimulus in a way that sensory input cannot. It is hard to conceptualize—meaning re-experience—pain; but it is easy to re-visualize a lemon. Obviously pain can be conceptualized verbally; but this conceptualization at a higher or symbolic level is akin to describing in words the re-visualized lemon. "Sensory" awareness may occur at a thalamic or limbic level, for sensory data may reach awareness as somatic or visceral sensations and also as affective valence or contribution to a percept, concept, memory, or anticipation. Percepts require cortical participation—particularly the primary projection area and adjacent areas. Conceptualization, the next level of input processing, may occur in the absence of concrete external stimuli.

Conscious awareness means that an organism knows a stimulus is present. It is a phenomenon presumably common to many animals. It is mediated by cortical primary projection areas operating in parallel with the widespread non–modality-marked cortical consciousness system. Thus the conscious awareness is a manifestation of general cortical participation, and the something of which one is aware is a manifestation of the participation of specific cortical regions (the primary projection area and other related areas), which also participate in the modality nonspecific genesis of consciousness. Conscious awareness allows the facultative luxury of responding immediately, responding later, or not responding at all—and this can be done even without awareness of the awareness.

Awareness of awareness, the highest level of consciousness, is a human attribute that may be shared by some other animals and can be called self-consciousness. It is not consciousness of the self in terms of such things as body image, for evidence suggests that infants in whom cortical maturation has not yet occurred have knowledge of the body— that is, have a body image. Before development of awareness of awareness, the child can distinguish personal space from extrapersonal; so it is not consciousness of self in a physical sense. Rather, it is consciousness of itself, consciousness of consciousness, or a mental process recursively reflecting a mental process. It occurs only at the conceptual level.

These three levels of consciousness parallel the three types of consciousness posited by Tulving: 1) The "nonknowing" anoetic, which has "awareness of" (better termed "response to") stimuli; 2) The "knowing" noetic, which is aware of the representation of stimuli (percepts); and 3) The "selfknowing" autonoetic, which incorporates awareness of self.[3]

7

There Was the Word:
Self-Consciousness and Language

The question of whether nonhuman animals are conscious—for some students of nature believe they are not—highlights the ambiguities in the term consciousness. In the intransitive sense, animals are certainly conscious. Asleep or awake, they are able to respond to stimuli from their environment. In the transitive sense, response must be to *something* and implies an awareness of the thing, for the response is attractive or aversive, a movement toward or away from *the thing*. To get around the problem of awareness (really meaning conscious awareness or awareness of awareness), the response, at the simplest level, is termed a reflex, or a tropism. Tropism—a turning—is considered involuntary—without awareness, as in the turning of a plant towards a source of light (which assumes plants are unaware). In actuality, the responding animal must be aware not only of the presence or existence of the thing (the stimulus or percept) but also of the *meaning of the thing*, in terms of its biological significance. This meaning relates the percept to the structural or biological integrity of the entire organism.

The integrity of the entire organism brings up the notion of self as a physical entity and the psychological concept of self. Physically, the self is represented neurologically by the internal and middle environments, which are surrounded by a bag of skin in the case of highly evolved animals. But the external environment, transduced by the senses and registered in the central nervous system, can become part of that self in the same sense that memory becomes part of the individual, bridging the gap between the physical and psychological aspects of self. Clearly, evolved animals have a sense of personal space—of bodily boundaries. Their aversion to noxious stimuli indicates that. From this evolves the psychological sense of self. Animals project that sense of self onto extra personal space. Territoriality is a clear example. Dogs mark *their* extra personal space with urine and female redwings, in the absence of males, with song; maternal mammals protect *their* pups. This identification of what is *mine* presumes an awareness of *me*; for without a me, there can be no mine. Awareness of self and its double set of boundaries (personal and extrapersonal) is different from *recognition* of self, although the recognition of the external projection of self (for example, territory) may be easier than the recognition of the individual as represented in personal space. But the distinction of personal from extrapersonal space is not sharp, for a component of personal space (such as a leg) may be thrust into extrapersonal space, where it may be recognized as "mine" by an exteroceptive system (such as vision) functioning in external space. For the human (a visual organism), self-recognition may occur in the mirror. But for less evolved creatures, self-recognition is more often by smell (marking) or audition (bird song). The reflected image of the Siamese fighting fish apparently indicates a fighting fish but not self; and the monkey (as far as anyone can tell) does not recognize its own reflection.

Just as the question of nonhuman animal consciousness points out the ambiguities in the term consciousness, so the question of nonhuman animal language indicates the ambiguity of the term language. Language is as hard to define, as is consciousness; no satisfactory comprehensive definition exists. At the simplest level it is a symbol system modeling reality. But other symbol systems model reality, too; mathematics is an outstanding example. It is also a symbol system that can *create* reality. It can model things that do not exist, such as unicorns. Deconstructionists notwithstanding, fiction is not just words on paper; when read it *becomes* real. Pooh Bear is as much a part of remembered childhood as Kurtz is a part of later life. Fantasy (aesthetic or psychiatric) becomes part of psychic reality. Other symbol systems can create reality, too. I am told, for example, that Clerk Maxwell postulated the Heaviside layer before Heaviside described the ionosphere; and modern physics predicts entities still to be identified. Prediction is, after all, the creation of reality that does not yet exist. A symbol system permits the creation of reality because it can be detached from its referent. A percept requires the presence of the perceived object; but a concept, the product of a symbol system, is freed of this dependency.

To think of language only as a system of communication is overly restrictive. Certainly it *is* a system of communication, but other biological communication systems also exist. Pheromones, displays, warning calls, and threatening behavior all convey information and imply intent. Consider the dance of the honeybee. Often what is not said communicates as much information as what is said. So does lying, another linguistic creation of reality. It has been said that children do not acquire real language until they learn to lie. But language is not necessary for lying. There is a species of ants that can generate a pheromone indicating subjugation of an enemy ant even when such an event has not occurred.

Yet another function of language is to operate on the external environment, perhaps changing it or controlling it. "Come here," we tell a friend. "Stay," we tell the dog. "Whoa!" we tell the horse. "Damn you!" we say to the stool over which we have tripped. Was it Robert Graves who said that when we say how hot it is, we make the day

> *It is reasonable to suppose that self-consciousness requires some system of symbols for its realization.*

seem cooler? (See page 135.) The operation is even more subtle, for linguistic formulation may change, or may condition what we perceive or experience. This linguistic operation may also operate on the internal environment, providing access to memory. Asked to visualize the face of your first sweetheart, you will probably subvocally articulate a name as an access to the proper address in visual storage. Or the linguistic formulation may plan—even indirectly—the motor performance and give access to the motor program. Time and again I have watched (say) a distinguished, dignified gentleman in a pinstripe suit and wingtip shoes enter a crowded elevator and say, to no one in particular, "three" before pushing the button for the third floor. With that linguistic token he retrieves, perhaps from procedural memory, a complex motor pattern allowing him to proceed with his motor performance. I suspect the articulated "three" is an otherwise rare overt manifestation of a common type of subvocal verbalization. But this kind of language is not necessary for access to memory; dogs retrieve buried bones; and squirrels and scrub jays store against the future, when they will have to remember.

The supposition that self-consciousness and language are uniquely human and do not exist in the nonhuman animals raises the possibility that the former (self-consciousness) requires the latter (language) for existence—or that, in some way, self-consciousness and language are conjoined. It is reasonable to suppose that self-consciousness requires some system of symbols for its realization. Awareness requires the percept, not a symbol of the percept (except insofar as the neural representation is a symbol). The neural representation of the percept, of which one is aware, is a model. Awareness of awareness (self-consciousness) is a representation of that representation, a model of the model, a concept of a percept. One part of the brain speaks to another, but the language system is almost certainly not the natural language of humans. So, in that sense, the development of self-consciousness does not depend on the development of natural language. This might be inferred from the loss of a sector of consciousness in the presence of neurological lesions that produce an agnosia for an agnosia. In those instances (say anosognosia with autotopagnosia), language, as expressed or interpreted by the affected individual, is usually unimpaired. Perhaps some symbol system, a putatively deep (really deeper than deep) structure for the surface structure of natural language, is impaired. This nonlinguistic, putatively deeper structure, which underlies natural language, is also the language by which one part of the brain speaks to another. It is the symbol system that underlies natural language, allowing the creation of self-consciousness. It is not enough to say that this symbol system consists of neural impulses. The neural impulse—produced by a component—must be organized into a program of a system, the output of which differs from the output of the component—the neuron. The impulse is organized into a code—a language—the meaning of which is certainly determined by spatial distribution in the brain and—perhaps—by the temporal pattern of impulses. This code (or language) underlies natural language and interacts with another code underlying speech (as distinct from language) and its articulatory movements or motor programs. In this formulation, although natural language models reality, an abnormality of language (aphasia), instead of causing an alteration of other methods of modeling reality (looking as evidenced by eye movements), becomes a manifestation of the abnormality of a deeper-lying symbol system responsible for visual modeling (say) as well as for the modeling of language. Unfortunately, in the aphasic patient there is no way to assess the concept of self or the existence of self-consciousness, because these must be evaluated linguistically. Nonlinguistic behavior cannot be used as a criterion, because response to a percept or motor program based on procedural memory may signify awareness without indicating awareness of awareness.

8

See Here: Attention

A comparison of attention and consciousness offers some interesting parallels. Attention is defined as "the composite of different capacities or processes that reflect how stimuli are received and processed. It can be sustained or tonic, as in the case of vigilance; or it can be phasic, in which attention shifts to changing stimuli."[1] This could be called the definition of consciousness in which "vigilance" represents the intransitive state of consciousness and the shifting phase signifies transitive consciousness or awareness. This is emphasized by Steriade's remark about the presence of fast oscillations "during all states of vigilance including NREM sleep . . ."[2] It equates with the presence of the conscious state—the ability to act— during NREM sleep. There are other similarities as well. The reticular formation of the brain stem plays a role in attention just as it does in the conscious state.[3] Unattended stimuli are processed just as consciousness of unaware percepts exists.[4] The distinction I suggest between consciousness and awareness (of a percept, for example) is paralleled by the site–source distinction in the attention system. "By the *source* of attention we mean those anatomical areas that seem to be specific to attention, not primarily involved in other forms of processing. However, when attention operates during task performance, it will operate at the neural areas (*site* of attention) where the computations involved in the task are usually performed" (original italics).[5] The analogy with the modular organization of consciousness, perhaps by a different configuration of laminar connections of the perceptual modules, is suggested by increased blood flow to cortical areas concerned with "the passive registration of the same information."[6] This is reinforced by the observation that "attention-related modulations of the sensory-evoked activity in visual cortex reflected changes in input processing in extrastriate visual cortex . . ."[7] Although on initial analysis one might conclude there is no counterpart in the consciousness system for endogenous and exogenous attention, this may be more of a terminological distinction than a physiological one. Endogenous attention is described as under voluntary (here's that word again) control, but exogenous attention is reflexive (another ambiguous term) in response to external events that automatically capture attention. In the consciousness system, after all, there are certain events that capture awareness and others of which we are conscious (aware) only as the result of concerted effort. "Considerable evidence indicates that without attention, conscious perception cannot occur."[8] Furthermore, reflexive attention has been shown to "modulate early visual processing at the same neural locus as voluntary attention";[9] and the notion of selective or focused attention (defined as the cognitive function allowing the focusing of processing resources onto the sensory inputs relevant in a given context) with the simultaneous withdrawal from the irrelevant does not help in the distinction from selective conscious awareness.[10] Finally, gamma oscillations, which are postulated to result in the formation of neural assemblies that underlie consciousness, are alleged to be significant in focused attention as well as in the perceptual binding of consciousness.[11] Although we do not want to blur the boundaries that define turfs, an economical multidisciplinary approach might explore the similarities—rather than the differences—between attention (in at least two senses) and consciousness (in two senses).

9

Perchance to Dream: Sleep

Many discussions of consciousness deal with sleep as a state in which consciousness is suspended or does not exist, a consequence of the equation of consciousness with awareness. Searle, for example, says, "Until you fall asleep again or otherwise become unconscious"— although, like Edelman, he excludes sleep with dreams.[1] Much can be learned about consciousness in an examination of sleep in human and nonhuman animals, despite the argument by some that consciousness does not exist in nonhuman species. If nonhumans are accepted as conscious, they can be used to address the postulate of the unity of consciousness; for some nonhumans—those as elevated in the evolutionary hierarchy as are dolphins or other whales—sleep with only one cerebral hemisphere at a time. So, if consciousness is unified, it is so for only a single hemisphere and for a lateral field—a point of some relevance with respect to anosognosia and autotopagnosia for a lateralized limb.

Wakefulness—as opposed to sleep—is alertness or vigilance, which raises again the relation between vigilance (or attention) and consciousness. But vigilance has been attributed not only to wakefulness but also to slow-wave sleep. The antithesis—sleep—is not a unified entity (in a somewhat different sense from the unity of consciousness) but is divided into levels. Consciousness, too, may be graded, but its levels are not defined by objective criteria (unless you agree that sleep is a phase of consciousness). As is true for consciousness, sleep behavior, too, may not be an adequate criterion of the internal state. As Ernest Hartman pointed out, one may ask a sleeper, "Are you sleeping?"—but only if the answer is "yes" can you judge the verbal behavior to be distinct from the internal state.

Sleep can be divided into two major phases. The first is characterized by rapid eye movement (REM), muscle atonia (except eye and respiratory muscles) resulting from inhibition of spinal alpha motor neurons, dreaming, and electrographic activity that resembles wakefulness. The brain is active, but the body is paralyzed. The electrographically active brain accounts for the term "paradoxical sleep" that is applied to this REM state.

The second phase is characterized by lack of rapid eye movement (non-REM or NREM), preserved muscle tone accompanied by episodic movements of postural readjustment, unawareness of most sensations (except for fragments of dreams in deepest sleep), and electrographic changes divided into four stages demarcating non-REM depths of sleep. Stage 1, often thought to coincide with the onset of sleep, exhibits fast, low-voltage activity with loss of posteriorly located alpha activity (about 10 cps) present when the subject is awake but has closed eyes. Stage 2 reveals spindles and K complexes characteristic of sleep. In Stages 3 and 4 are increasing delta (1–4 Hz), or slow-wave, activity, giving rise to the term "slow-wave sleep." Delta waves reflect hyperpolarization of thalamic relay cells. NREM sleep is said to indicate an "inactive" brain in a mobile body. (Obviously inactive is a poorly chosen term if the body is mobile; the mobility indicates brain activity.) The "inactivity" reflects a blockade of thalamic afferent activity. REM and NREM sleep periods cycle during the night. REM and NREM comprise roughly 90-minute epochs; but as the night progresses, the cycles consist of longer REM periods. Interestingly, REM sleep and its consciousness (of dreams) is presumed by some to be at a deeper level than Stage 4's "unconscious," slow-wave sleep. In slow-wave sleep there is obliteration of thalamic transmission with deafferentation of cortex and persistence of corticocortical and corticothalamic conduction.

Knowledge of the anatomical substate of sleep may contribute to the understanding of consciousness

Knowledge of the anatomical substate of sleep may contribute to the understanding of consciousness—whether or not one considers sleepers to be conscious. A prominent part is played by the hypothalamus, a paired multinuclear structure on either side of the midline, atop the brain stem, and below the thalamus. Cell groups from the brain stem (part of the ascending arousal system) project to the lateral hypothalamus and are joined by axons from other areas. The ventrolateral preoptic nucleus of the hypothalamus sends inhibitory fibers to the brain stem arousal nuclei (which, in turn, project widely to the thalamus and cortex), becoming instrumental in the promotion of sleep. This emphasizes, once again, the role of the ascending reticular activating system (broad sense) in the genesis of consciousness—whether or not one considers slow-wave sleep a conscious state.

That it is a conscious state can be inferred from both normal and abnormal sleep behavior. In normal sleep, sleepers are more likely to be aroused by the soft enunciation of their names than by the name of another; similarly, a sleeping mother may respond to the cry of her own baby while ignoring the cry of an unrelated infant. In these situations some sensory processing must take place, and some percept formation must occur, without awareness (and often without memory)—underscoring that awareness need not be necessary for perception or for consciousness.[2]

The functions of sleep are still not understood. Among the suggestions so far proposed are that sleep replenishes energy lost to increased metabolic demands during periods of wakefulness, for the brain's metabolism is lowered during sleep. Sleep also has been thought to enhance the activity of the immune system. A third suggestion is that sleep is important in reinforcing connections between neurons—a view at odds with the suggestion of a breakdown of connections during sleep. During wakefulness, transcranial magnetic stimuli (nonphysiologic stimuli) spread to connected cortical areas several centimeters away; during NREM sleep, the response does not propagate beyond the stimulus site. A similar cognitive unbinding is thought to occur in the case of anesthesia. Of particular interest concerning the issue of consciousness is the consolidation of learning reported to occur during sleep. Following training in a task thought to involve the right parietal cortex, human subjects during NREM sleep increased slow-wave activity only in the appropriate area; and, later, when awake, showed improved performance in the learned task.

Finally there is the question of consciousness in sleep-related behavior disorders, some of which occur during REM. In these the characteristic atonia of the REM state is lacking, allowing dream-enhancing behavior such as running or attack. Sleepwalking, sleeptalking, sleepeating, and night terrors may be highly structured activities occurring during electrographic slow-wave sleep. That REM sleep and dreaming may follow Stage 4 slow-wave sleep does not mean that REM is "deep sleep." But, even if REM is considered light sleep (as implied by subjects' ease of arousal), the existence of dream imagery fragments and dream-like mentation in Stages 3 and 4 supports the contention that consciousness persists during sleep. It is unlikely that consciousness would be suspended in the early stages of sleep only to return in the deepest of all.

Sleep behavior disorders, learning consolidation during NREM sleep, response to selected external stimuli, and dreaming in the deepest sleep states—all argue for the persistence of consciousness in sleep and the disjunction of consciousness and awareness.

10

$x=2y$:
Representation

More than one hundred years ago, Hughlings Jackson suggested that information represented at one level of the nervous system was re-represented at another and re-re-represented at yet a third. This is true for such fundamental functions as movement, which is initially represented in the spinal cord and re-represented in the brain stem and at even higher levels. At each level of representation, modification occurs. The coarse response of low levels is increasingly refined (individuated, in Coghill's terminology), ultimately reaching digital delicacy in movement. Similar re-representation occurs on the input side. This reiteration of motor phenomena or of sensory and perceptual input suggests that recursion is a general principle of neurological organization, occurring ultimately in such high-level performances as language (which can conceptualize in the absence of a perceptual stimulus) and consciousness of consciousness.

Interesting questions are: how much cortex is necessary for conscious awareness? If there is a critical amount, how does this come about? Are there varying amounts of conscious awareness from individual to individual just as there are varying amounts of cerebral cortex?

Discussion of the amount of cortex necessary for conscious awareness must be divided into two parts—one for consciousness and a second for awareness. If the early decortication studies are accurate, cortex is not necessary for consciousness; but decorticate consciousness would be consciousness at the lowest level. Generated in the brain stem by modality-nonspecific input to the reticular activating system, it also sends information downstream to the spinal cord to facilitate spinal reflexes. In contrast, the awareness part of conscious awareness requires a cortical component at least for perceptual awareness. Sensory awareness of pain and other primary modalities probably does not require cortex; it takes place at a thalamic level. For perceptual awareness, appropriate primary projection areas (such as visual cortex for vision and sensory cortex for somesthetic sensation) must be functioning. It is probable that some of the appropriate association areas are also required both for the formulation of the percept and for awareness of its existence. In addition, an attentive component must be present. Whether the mechanism of that attention is separate from that of the consciousness part of conscious awareness is not evident. One major distinction, however, is that attention can be focused or lateralized (as evident in behavior subsequent to cerebral lesions) in contrast with consciousness, the lateralization of which may occur—but is hard to demonstrate.

Because most input-output systems in the cerebrum are crossed, contralateral space is represented in the primary projection areas. Of interest is the fact that olfaction, conducted by a primitive system, is not crossed. It may be no coincidence that of all the sensory modalities, olfactory input is the most difficult to localize in space. Representation of reality (particularly the external environment encoded by the teloreceptors) is sharply delimited at the midline in the primary projection areas. A lesion of right visual cortex obliterates the left visual field in each eye (although the macula is spared). Right parietal lesions affect sensation in the left body. The world is divided at the midline, yet we do not experience the world as consisting of two halves. The fusion takes place in the cortical areas beyond the primary projection cortices in the ongoing chain of projection. The visual field, for example, embraces both sides of space, as represented in each temporal lobe of a monkey.

The unsatisfactory notion of cerebral dominance can be clarified, perhaps, by relating it to the midline. Customarily employed in discussing language (most often the left hemisphere is dominant for language production and comprehension) it also relates to handedness and, undoubtedly, to other entities. Often it is defined as "ease of learning"—"the left hemisphere learns language more easily than the right." Not only is this not explanatory, but it further complicates the concept by introducing the notion of learning. Classically, dominance is determined by the effects of a cerebral lesion (although other methods are available), a deficit of function indicating the lesioned hemisphere to be dominant for that function. A more satisfactory way of looking at dominance, in my view, is that a dominant function crosses the midline so that a unilateral lesion produces a bilateral deficit. In that formulation, dominance is not limited to language or handedness, does exist for a large number of cerebral functions, and is not uniquely human. How it comes about is not clear, but some interesting evidence suggests that peripheral input is responsible. Years ago, the Russians claimed to be able to determine which hemisphere would become dominant for language by manipulating a hand of a newborn or very young infant. Cerebral representation of the hand is widespread over cortex bilaterally in early life. With manipulation, they claimed, the area of representation of the hand, as determined by electroencephalographic recording, coalesces into an increasingly smaller focus, "making room" for the language function to develop. Handedness is another case in point. Studying the effect of penetrating wartime head injuries, the Mount Sinai group concluded that position sense in the fingers was diminished—as expected—in the hand opposite the lesioned non-dominant hemisphere but was diminished in both hands with a lesioned dominant hemisphere.

This duplication of function across the midline in a single hemisphere raises again the question of relationship between attention and consciousness (in the basic sense). In contrast to the lateralized input from the lemniscal systems, which retain the imprint of laterality all the way to cortex, the input to and output from the reticular activating system lose indication of modality and laterality. Basic consciousness is without lateral field of reference. The attention function, as determined by effects of lesions, is lateralized. Not only can attention be focused, but the lesioned organism can be deprived of attention to one half of the environment (or field). This is most evident when the deprivation is caused by a lesion in the hemisphere opposite the one dominant for language. Years ago it was suggested that consciousness was represented in the hemisphere dominant for language. If that formulation has any validity, it could be argued that consciousness is but a bilateral manifestation of attention represented in dominant hemisphere, while lateralized attention (as determined by inattention) is a non-dominant function that does not cross the midline.

Lateralized inattention, which has been demonstrated for many modalities, is most easily demonstrated in the visual or somesthetic spheres and brings to the fore the problem that conscious awareness (or attention) must be directed to something—a percept. The issue then becomes whether the loss of awareness caused by a lesion affects the attention-consciousness system—or whether it affects the percept instead. It further raises the problem of unconsciousness awareness.

With certain right-hemisphere lesions, visual neglect of the left field may occur. The patient can see in that field and, when stimulated uniquely in the left field, can correctly report the stimulus. When a simultaneous visual stimulus occurs in the right field, the left stimulus may not be reported—presumably indicating that the subject is not aware of having seen it. Unilateral neglect of left personal space can be demonstrated to touch when homologous parts on both sides are touched simultaneously, even though the single stimulus on either side is appreciated. Bilateral appreciation of touch can be restored by increasing the size (hand on left, fingertip on right) or duration (fingertip long time on left, fingertip short time on right) of the left body stimulus. Thus the perceptual rivalry can be overcome by spatial or temporal summation. The similarity to the response to subliminal stimuli is emphasized by the fact that visual stimuli in the neglected field may influence a response to visual stimuli in the intact field.[1]

What makes this of particular interest is that in the normal, non-lesioned individual, reducing the size or duration of a stimulus (best shown in the visual system) can remove it from awareness. Thus there is a minimal discriminable spatial size or interval in vision, and a minimal duration, required for visual stimulus to reach conscious awareness. Lacking that duration, a visual percept is not reported. This suggests that conscious awareness can be altered in normal subjects by manipulation of the thing (the percept) of which one is aware without manipulating the consciousness factor—which is presumably mediated widely and not controlled by the size or duration of the specific stimulus. This reduction in size or duration of a stimulus to an amount at which awareness disappears is the negative of spatial and temporal summation, a result of spatial and temporal subtraction.

The difficulty of separating the percept from awareness of it results from the fact that the input of both to the cerebral hemisphere is usually crossed. If there were an uncrossed modality, the relation to awareness could be disentangled; and olfaction provides such an opportunity, for the olfactory system is uncrossed—perhaps accounting for the difficulty in spatially locating fragrance in contrast to vision or touch. Double simultaneous olfactory stimulation in patients with left unilateral neglect attendant on a right-hemisphere lesion demonstrated neglect of the olfactory stimulus in the left nostril. In theory, the odor is decoded by the left hemisphere, but the awareness of it (as indicated by the negative effect of a lesion) is the responsibility of the right hemisphere.[2] Thus the sensation or percept is dissociated from awareness of it with respect to the locus (and therefore the presumed mechanism) of representation.

The complication relates to the inclusion in the nostril of trigeminal (crossed) innervated epithelium as well as olfactory (uncrossed) epithelium. If there is altered awareness of the (crossed) nostril and its trigeminal epithelium, the disruption of sensation–awareness linkage may not be as clear-cut as the experimental results suggest.

We speak of subliminal stimuli—an obvious contradiction in terms. Stimulus is defined by response (no response, no stimulus), and response is defined by the associated neural activity, whether with or without awareness or overt behavioral manifestation. When we speak of subliminal stimulus, it is really the response that is subliminal—by which we mean subliminal for awareness. The stimulus that evokes a subliminal response is clearly not subliminal. The paradox is that the subject may be aware of the response (behavior) while unaware of the precipitant—the stimulus—or its initial response (for example, volition as the initial instantiation of the neural response that ultimately generates behavioral action). This subliminal response (such as not "seeing" a very brief visual stimulus, for "seeing" is a response) is of importance in the analysis of the neural activation that precedes awareness of volition and the subsequent action that volition "produces." It is as if the neural response, like the stimulus, must have a certain duration to become "liminal" for awareness—or, to put it differently, the initial, subliminal neural response becomes the stimulus for the emergent property "awareness."

An interesting outcome that follows from all of this is the possibility that generalized cortical consciousness is not a continuum but rather a mosaic. Each contributing fragment of generalized consciousness is tightly linked to the perceptual network from which it comes. Projected in parallel, the percept and the consciousness of it can be impaired separately. If only the perceptual component is destroyed, conscious awareness of it is lost but the nonperceptual component of the network can continue to contribute to generalized consciousness. If only the consciousness component is destroyed, conscious awareness of the percept may be impaired—as evidenced by inattention produced by lesions—but perception can be restored by recruiting additional fragments from the consciousness mosaic by means of temporal or spatial summation.

Projected in parallel, the percept and the consciousness of it can be impaired separately.

If the subliminal stimulation studies are accurate, behavior can be determined by percepts that are not perceived—that do not come to conscious awareness. But if behavior can be controlled by subliminal stimulation, there must be awareness at some level, raising questions about unconscious awareness and creating the need for a hierarchy of unconsciousness—just as there is a hierarchy of consciousness. Behavior control (of which the subject is unaware) by stimuli (also of which the subject is unaware) becomes—in the hierarchy of unconsciousness— the analog of self-consciousness; that is, unawareness of unawareness, an entity to be confronted again in discussion of agnosia for an agnosia. Stated differently, this subliminal phenomenon in normal subjects mimics pathological behavior subsequent to a lesion.

One way to conceive of the genesis of conscious awareness is as a threshold function. Threshold can be understood in one of two ways. The first is exemplified by a drinking tumbler slowly filling under a dripping tap. At the point the tumbler begins to overflow the threshold has been reached. The input and output are identical in quantity and quality at any given moment, producing a steady state. Inherent in the second type of threshold—and of interest in relation to the genesis of consciousness—is a limen at which an abrupt, rapid, qualitative change occurs. This is a familiar biological occurrence that also exists in physical and mechanical systems. A steady lowering of the temperature of water continues until, suddenly, at threshold, a rapid change occurs. Water disappears and a new entity appears—ice. In the mechanical sphere an example would be an aircraft that steadily gains ground speed until, at the critical moment—threshold—it is airborne, moving faster and in a new mode. In biology this is well known in such entities as the S-shaped oxygen dissociation curve of hemoglobin or the categorical perception of phonemes. More pertinent to neurological systems is the well-known increase of generator potential in response to a linear increase of stimulus intensity until a sudden transition at threshold produces a self-propagating action potential the amplitude of which is independent of stimulus amplitude.

There is reason to believe that cerebral modular structures exist in cortex and thalamus. In cortex, though widely distributed, they are related. Columnar in architecture, they can contain as few as 110 cells. They may be interconnected and are the distributed anatomical basis of a distributed function—a rather different concept from the alleged centers of function claimed by the localizationists. "A thalamic nucleus is organized in a columnar manner in the sense that the flow of impulses from an afferent input through a thalamic relay cell is segregated from impulses flowing through other thalamic relay cells."[3] Cortical conscious awareness can be viewed as coming into being when a threshold number of widely distributed modules aggregates to function as a unit. Suddenly a phenomenon that does not inhere within an individual module, or even within a cohort of a few such, emerges, widely distributed—as is its anatomical substrate. Speculation is that relatively few modules are required to reach threshold and create the emergent property of conscious awareness, in light of the surprisingly small number of cells that can form a cortical column. Unresolved, of course, is the question of whether this is part of the percept system or is a separate system operating in parallel in the way the autonomic system, the postural adjustment system, and the limbic affective system operate in parallel with each other and with modality-specific input to cortex underlying percept formation.

There is no reason however why it cannot be both—part of the percept system and a separate system simultaneously. Widely dispersed modules can be assembled differently. Using the same modules, differing configurations of networks can be obtained if modules receive modality-specific and modality–non-specific inputs in different layers of the module—not a farfetched idea in view of the knowledge that specific thalamic afferents terminate in granular layer four of six-layered cortex; some nonspecific input terminates in superficial layer one; and layers two and three send projections to other cortical areas, perhaps creating different assemblies from the same modules. Different assemblies of modules can be conceived to emphasize different aspects of the modular cortical column. One configuration in which layer four figures prominently subserves, at threshold, the percept. A second network, configuring the same modules differently and perhaps adding additional modules, emphasizes the nonspecific input to the columns and contributes, at threshold, to the genesis of consciousness. In the visual system, it has been shown that cellular response to visual stimuli is similar whether the animal is asleep or awake. With wakefulness, however, the activity of layers five and six increases, although there is little change of activity of the upper layers. This raises the possibility that assemblies based on configuration of layer four are concerned with perception and that assemblies structured on configurations of layers five and six subserve awareness.

Self-consciousness, in this formulation, occurs at a higher (that is, later phylogenetic) level and is concept- rather than percept-based. As such, it can operate independent of physically present stimulus and can function even outside the realm of physical reality. Awareness of awareness requires some symbol system, such as language, in order to specify the awareness of which the self is aware. This raises the unresolved question of how one part of the brain talks to the other parts. It is surely not in a natural language such as English, but it could be isomorphic (in the mathematical sense of the term) with a natural language. The requirement for an internal symbol system probably indicates that most nonhuman animals lack self-consciousness, despite the evidence that great apes can be taught an artificial symbol system.[4]

The paradox is that the brain cannot experience itself as an organ. Part of the inner environment, it cannot participate as part of the inner environment. Unlike other viscera (the brain, too, is a hollow organ) the brain is not endowed with interoceptors. It cannot represent itself. It models the world other than itself. Its model of reality is not isomorphic (in the biological sense of the term) with the world represented. There is no homunculus—a real little man—in the brain. Whatever way the world is inscribed in brain can at one level become a stimulus input for another level. Perceptual images (in the broad sense of the word) can become input to conceptual levels. The brain's model of reality becomes part of the input environment on which other parts of the brain operate. Thus the brain becomes part of the environment while simultaneously operating on that part of the environment.

It is worth recalling Sherrington's description of divergence at this point. Output from a single nerve cell may be distributed by its axon terminals to several other nerve cells, which, if activated, can (by multiple axon terminals) distribute the output of the original cell—now modified by the intervening cells—widely in the central nervous system. This divergence may be geographic as well as physiologic. The ultimate output need not be aggregated. Indeed, evidence at the most fundamental level—the motor unit—as well as at the highest level—cerebral cortex— suggests wide dispersion. A single motor neuron, innervating a collection of muscle fibers, does so over a wide territory. The muscle fibers are not aggregated in a bundle but are interspersed between the muscle fibers of other motor units. This low-level plan of structure and function is repeated throughout the neuraxis up to the level of cortex. This should not be taken to mean there are no anatomical nuclear aggregates or that there is no geographic grouping of physiologic function. It does mean, however, that a function, such as vision, that is located in the occipital lobe at the back part of the brain is also represented elsewhere (the temporal and parietal lobes, at least), and widely so.

Lesions at various levels of the neuraxis release postures. Flexion is the predominant posture following spinal injury, extension with lower brain stem lesions, and flexion again with section of the higher brain stem. The flexor spasm, or triple flexion response, evoked by a noxious stimulus may persist for long periods after the presumed stimulus has been removed. It may be evoked by interoceptors (a full or infected urinary bladder) as well as by proprioceptors or exteroceptors. The prolonged position suggests that it may be posture that is represented at various neural levels, coupled with a transition mechanism allowing a small shift to the next represented posture. According to this view, movement consists of static positions with transition from one posture to the next. This is the analog, on the output side, of the visual "snapshots" sequenced by a generalized cinematographic brain mechanism to create the illusion of movement on the input side.

Rigid extension of the extremities—the opposite of flexor spasm—is released by lesions at brain stem levels. When isolation occurs above the vestibular nuclei but below the red nucleus, a posture of extension of limbs and body is sufficiently intense to allow the decerebrate quadriped to stand. Vestibular input is necessary to sustain this decerebrate rigidity. Several aspects of the vestibular system should be noted: 1) It is the lowest-level input system above the spinal cord. Its brain stem nuclei are served by the eighth cranial nerve. 2) It is an extremely old system, having evolved from the lateral line organ of fish. 3) It supplies a major proprioceptive input of which the human organism is unaware until imbalance occurs. As such, it is an example of what is here termed afferent. 4) Imbalance can occur because the paired organ (one on each side) functions as a null indicator, one side canceling the effect of the other so long as they beat symmetrically. When one side becomes more (or less) active than the other, the imbalance and illusion of motion come to awareness. 5) The end organs in the inner ear beat tonically so they are always active. Phasic change alters the tonic output, which, because it is always present, serves as an important source of input to the consciousness system. 6) Despite the fact there is no awareness of the normally functioning vestibular system, it is widely represented in cerebral cortex (particularly in cats which have a remarkable way of landing on their feet from any initial posture—but only if the vestibule is intact). This representation is not at the perceptual level—there is no conscious awareness—yet it is there operating in parallel with percepts and contributing to the conscious part of conscious awareness.

To rapidly conclude this discussion of representation, re-representation, and re-re-representation of motor function (or modeling, remodeling, and re-remodeling of motor output), the flexion of spinal origin is modified by input from the red nucleus of the upper brain stem into flexion of major parts of a member.

Extension, I suspect, is re-represented in subcortical nuclei (witness the flexed posture of the patient with Parkinson's disease of the idiopathic variety—paralysis agitans—whose striatal system is impaired). Finally, digital finesse appears with cortical input.

The issue of reorganization of function at ascending levels of neuraxis can be observed another way. Stimulation at any motor level of the intact organism, from cortex to motor root, evokes motion. With cortical stimulation, an organized movement—the conjunction of action by many muscles—occurs. With ventral (motor) root stimulation, a single muscle or muscle fascicle contracts. Stimulation at levels between reveals varying organization of muscle participation.

Seen from the negative aspect of loss of function, a cortical lesion may indeed inflict such a loss in a muscle—such as latissimus dorsi—when a cerebrally initiated movement, such as adduction of the arm, is required. Loss of function may also be demonstrated when the patient attempts to cough voluntarily in response to a command. But a cough evoked by a tickle of the throat actively innervates the previously paralyzed muscle, indicating representation of movement, not muscle, at high levels, and demonstrating that one stimulus may be adequate when another is not.

Posture and movement deserve the attention we have given them because they are ancient phylogenetic phenomena out of which a great deal has evolved. Movement signals the presence of another animal. It is appreciated at several visual levels and serves to orient the animal to the visual field. Even at the relatively peripheral station of the retinal ganglion cell movement is recorded—"bug receptor of the frog." In recovery of visual loss following a cerebral lesion, movement may be appreciated long before the moving object can be recognized—a situation familiar to the normal individual, who is often aware of movement in the far peripheral field (as in a traffic intersection) before being aware of the object that is moving. But objects may be seen and perception of movement disturbed. The dissociation of the two relates to the existence of two separate pathways in the visual system.

Movement lies at the root of many human capabilities. "It is through action that we become conscious of ourselves."[3] A case might even be made that cognition grew out of movement. Animal behavior—whatever else it may be—is movement. Movement is the fundamental component of communication systems, whether body language or speech. Indeed, it could be argued that all movement is communication—that it bears a message. It signals not only a presence but also a state. It is an intentional signal system for such things as baring of teeth but is also an unintentional communication system. For example, spinal walking exists, but by the time the nervous system is fully developed, the way one walks is conditioned by generational, ethnic, and situational—including emotional—factors. We stride, stroll, or saunter; we promenade, hike, or tramp; we march, pace, or hurry. Each has a different meaning and conveys a different message to observers. Behaviorism may be out of fashion, but—as Sherrington noted—the mind (of another) is always an inference from behavior. Consciousness, like mind, is a very private affair. It is made manifest by the only overt product of the nervous system—movement.

12

They All Fall Down: Dissolution of Function

Lesions of the nervous system have a long history of use in exploring the structure and function of the brain. Morphological changes following injury help identify tracts and cell bodies. Physiologic impairment helps clarify functional organization. A strong word of caution is needed, however, in each category. Anatomically, tract degeneration is of limited value in comparison with newer techniques, and retrograde cell degeneration studies give incomplete information when compared to more recent staining techniques.

Functionally, the caution is even more important, for there are fewer more technically advanced methods to supplant the use of lesions than are found in the anatomical category. Positron emission tomography scans and functional magnetic resonance imaging studies give a static picture of an isolated moment in what is usually an artificially structured, created situation.[1] That is, it does not truly reflect the biological stimuli of the world in which we live. More important, indication of cerebral activity (usually blood flow) by these techniques reveals regions of emphasis of activity but not necessarily the full distribution—either at the cortical or lower levels. The difficulty is compounded when accepting the notion of emergent properties, for the imaging techniques cannot trace a property. They can demonstrate brain areas of increased blood flow—and, therefore, of *presumed* neuronal activity. The neuronal activity results in increased metabolism, increased carbon dioxide production, and vascular dilatation—and, therefore, increased blood flow. But though, as the philosophers emphasized, neuronal activity may underlie and correlate with a property, it is not the property. An analogy may help, clumsy though it be. A pool of water tagged with a radioisotope can be located with a counter, but the counter cannot determine the state (property) of the substance in the pool—water or ice. Finally, the problem is that imaging cannot separate consciousness, in the sense of readiness or arousal, from the thing of which the subject is conscious—the content, percept, or sensation: this is the ambiguity inherent in the term consciousness.

In behavior studies performed after cerebral lesions, several major points, though often neglected, must be considered when evaluating the effects of an ablation. The behavioral effects of a lesion are operationally defined. It has been said that an operational definition tells more about the measuring device than it does about the entity being measured. If we measure the behavioral alteration, we are in possession of it as a concept; if we do not measure it, it eludes us. This is dramatically demonstrated in the study of aphasia, a disorder of language attendant on a lesion of the so-called dominant hemisphere, usually in the posterior superior temporal lobe. A study of the eye movements—looking—of aphasic patients in response to a nonverbal stimulus reveals a chaotic pattern of visual fixation suggesting an abnormality in "seeing." For example, an outline drawing of a pitcher of water held above a partially filled glass—but lacking the stream of water from pitcher to tumbler—evokes a stream of macular fixation points following the course of the absent stream when viewed by a normal individual. The pattern of looking fills in the stream and indicates that the subject knows it should be there. In response to the same drawing, the aphasic patient looks first here, then there, within the pitcher or glass, at the borders of the drawing—haphazardly. This looking pattern in response to a nonlinguistic stimulus (for the subject is told nothing but simply looks) suggests an abnormality in modeling the visual world of a patient with aphasia. Thus aphasia becomes a disorder not of language in isolation (caused by a lesion to a "language center"), but part of a generalized disorder of neural modeling of reality, of which language (one function of which is to model reality) is the spearhead. The usual operational definition of aphasia obtained by measuring language alone does not reveal this.

The problem of operational definition is put into bold relief when used to define consciousness. Customarily behavioral criteria (i.e. movement) are used. "The operational index of consciousness is the ability to report."[2] An immobile patient—one who cannot indicate consciousness by reporting (movement)—is often presumed not conscious. Once again the inadequacy of behavior as criterion is realized, for behavior (spinal withdrawal as an example) can occur in the absence of consciousness, and, conversely, lack of behavior (as in the so-called vegetative state) need not mean lack of consciousness. In exploring the question of consciousness in the vegetative state, imaging has provided a new operation (other than behavior) by which to define consciousness. Functional magnetic resonance imaging of the brain of a young woman in a persistent vegetative state for five months revealed semantic disambiguation of spoken sentences and what might be construed as revisualization (or at least conceptualization) in response to imagining playing tennis or visiting all the rooms of her house. Accepting as three psychological attributes of consciousness: 1) Active maintenance of mental representations; 2) Strategic processing; and 3) Spontaneous intentional behavior, imaging studies provide the operation to assess #1 when #3 is lacking and so provide a new operational definition of consciousness.[3]

> *The problem of operational definition is put into bold relief when used to define consciousness.*

Lesions are a negative process—they take something away. Any activity that arises consequent to the lesion must be based elsewhere and not in the removed tissue. The new positive phenomenon is released or behaviorally disinhibited. The dictum is that negative lesions do not contain positive phenomena. Negative lesions produce negative effects such as a loss of vision in the contralateral field subsequent to an injury of the visual cortex. The released positive effects are a negation of behavioral inhibition (which is also a negation) by higher levels. In the study of alteration of consciousness attendant on cerebral lesions, only the negative effect can be studied, for (as far as can be told) consciousness does not have an inhibiting action on lower-represented processes. These become evident in attempts to assess loss of conscious awareness and become even more evident when related to self-consciousness, the absence of which—in any given sphere—is a negation of the negative (or absent) conscious awareness.

The presence of a lesion changes the context of the observed activity. Goldstein emphasizes this by pointing out that the lesioned organism is not a normal organism missing the function that was represented in the area of damage. Rather, it is a new organism functioning at optimal capability. The organism with a lesion of visual cortex on one side does not have a blind field on the contralateral side—although that is how we define it operationally. Rather, it has a full field half as large as the original. Thus, it is with consciousness—or, at least, with attention. As Kinsbourne points out, subsequent to a lesion causing unawareness, "in neglect the arena of consciousness itself has shrunk on one side; the patient who neglects a part of space or of his body does not experience the fact that he is neglecting it. Inattention to left-sided events itself shrinks the field of awareness."[4] The notion of context applies spectacularly (because the disconnection is so extensive) in the case of split-brain preparations. In humans with intractable epilepsy, section of the corpus callosum—the major commissural connection—has been performed in the past to prevent spread of epilepsy. Although other connections between hemispheres persist, the major bundle connecting homologous cortical areas (not all cortical areas get callosal connections) has been interrupted. It is now possible to study some functions of each hemisphere in isolation, but the demonstration of a behavior by the isolated hemisphere does not allow the conclusion that such behavior normally resides in that hemisphere when it is in the intact brain. One hemisphere, operating in the context of the other, probably receives multiple modulating inputs to shape the behavior rather differently from that which occurs when that hemisphere operates in isolation. An illustrative analogy is this: Forward progress of the body in space can be performed with either leg alone by hopping; bipedal walking is not hopping with two legs. The action is changed because the context of the activity is changed. The function of one leg is different in the presence of the other precisely because of the presence of the other.

One other caution—perhaps one of lesser importance—relates to the changeability of the central nervous system, particularly in the young—during so-called critical periods. This plasticity is reflected in the genesis of new cells, new processes (dendrites), new synapses, and changing synaptic strengths, producing entities such as long-term potentiation. Recovery, insofar as it can be measured, can occur following cortical lesions. Cortical modules at a distance, with connections in place, can be made to function as part of a new assembly, helping to restore lost functions.

13

Been There, Done That: Experience

Experience is an important determinant of neural function and, particularly in the young, is reflected in morphology. This experience is also context—but in a temporal framework rather than a spatial. A spike train in a single axon is not the same in response to a second stimulus as it was in response to an identical first stimulus: perhaps because the second stimulus is not the same as the first, occurring in the context of the first (or perhaps the configuration of the spike train is not what encodes the information conveyed). Gertrude Stein tells us "a rose is a rose is a rose." The second rose is not the same as the first; for it has been modified linguistically and eidetically by the presence of the first and the third.

Even at the lowest level—the axon of a frog on a laboratory bench—the effect of experience can be demonstrated. The stimulus voltage required to generate an action potential is determined, the axon is subjected to a burst of tetanic stimulation, and then the initial step is repeated. After the tetanus, stimulus voltage necessary to generate an action potential has been reduced. This so-called post-tetanic potentiation (descriptive rather than explanatory) can be construed, in this artificial situation, as a low-level form of memory suggesting, once again, a hierarchical organization or recursion.

The dynamic effect of antecedent experience was demonstrated a century ago by experiments studying the effect of cortical stimulation. When a discrete region of motor cortex is stimulated electrically, a contralateral movement is obtained. Where the motor strip is stimulated determines what contralateral part moves. Point-to-point correspondence has been mapped, and a picture of a little man (or "homunculus") has been drawn, leading some to conclude the homunculus is represented in brain. Interestingly, the movement produced is determined by the starting posture, so the stimulation of a cortical motor area may on one occasion cause one movement and on another occasion another. Sherrington speaks of this as the functional instability of cortical motor points. If a point low down on the motor strip is stimulated, a movement of the contralateral thumb may occur. This point is labeled the thumb area. If a region high up on the motor strip is stimulated, a movement of the contralateral shoulder may be evoked. This cortical point is labeled the shoulder area. Now, if the thumb area is restimulated and, point by point, cortex intervening between it and the shoulder area is serially stimulated, each stimulus evokes a movement of the thumb until the restimulation of the shoulder area evokes a movement of thumb. Is this now the shoulder area or the thumb area? It depends on the history of the neural assembly and represents a form of functional plasticity that is not usually considered.

Finally, experience is not passively received by the organism. Even at low levels there is feedback onto the input system. In a physiologic sense, the central nervous system constantly operates on the environment even as the environment constantly operates on the central nervous system. Percepts are conditioned by previous percepts, by contemporary impulses from other nonperceptual levels, and by the broad range of experience stored in episodic memory (which may be part of the perceptual system). This kind of operation on perception lets me see faces in the clouds. Behaviorally, as well, the nervous system operates on the environment to change it. One of the major functions of the nervous system is to manipulate the world—even language does that—and the changed environment then operates again on the nervous system.

As perceptual experience alters subsequent perceptual experience, consciousness does not change subsequent consciousness (this cannot be described as conscious experience because the experience component—what is experienced—is perceptual). It is as if the consciousness component of the dyad is impregnable simply because its input is not modality-marked. Thus, qualitatively—from the viewpoint of consciousness—one input at any given moment is the same as any other input at any other moment.

14

Which Have Eyes and See Not: Stimulus Hierarchy

Customarily we think of cerebral (particularly cortical) lesions as depriving the organism of the function located there—a notion left over from the heyday of phrenology. In the motor sphere, where it can be studied most easily, a lesion does not deprive the subject of motion. What has changed is the nature of the stimulus that can evoke the motion. Some stimuli that were previously adequate to elicit a response no longer do so; but others still function. In the case of cortical lesions, the stimuli that lose their adequacy are usually transduced by the exteroceptors. Verbal commands may no longer function. "Show me your teeth" evokes no action; the face is paralyzed on one side. But, a moment later, an amusing event evokes a bilateral smile. That this is not a disorder of language comprehension is evidenced by the fact that the paralyzed arm unable to be raised to command does not move to catch a ball thrown toward it from the world outside, a nonverbal stimulus. But, if the chair in which the patient is sitting is unexpected tipped back rapidly, the "paralyzed" arm rises promptly and correctly in a movement of postural readjustment. Stimulus for this comes predominantly from the vestibular and proprioceptive systems.

The apparent paradox that a lesion inside the organism affects the environment of the outside world is not really a paradox, for what is affected in the cerebrum is that part of the nervous system that models the outside world. If the lesion is in that part of the cerebrum that models the middle environment—the subcortical nuclei—the input from the proprioceptive system loses its adequacy, but the exteroceptors continue to function. Thus the Parkinson's patient who is rigid and bradykinetic catches a ball thrown unexpectedly but tumbles backwards en bloc when tipped back suddenly.

On the input side of hemisphere function, a similar situation occurs. The "insensate" arm withdraws upon being pinched. The patient with an occipital lesion and associated hemianopia has a pupil that contracts to retinal illumination from the impaired field, may blink to threats from that side, and may also perceive motion. Does that patient see or not? This suggests that there are levels of seeing, just as there are levels of movement. This hierarchy of stimuli is organized by the nervous system according to the biological significance of the stimulus. Those at the lowest level are the most concrete, the most biologically significant in terms of bodily integrity and evoke an urgent response that operates at a low neural level. As the stimulus hierarchy is ascended, the stimulus becomes less concrete, and the response becomes less urgent, less obligatory, and—possibly—less immediate. At the highest level of this stimulus pyramid is the abstract stimulus, which, in the presence of a cerebral lesion, is the first to succumb. This is particularly evident in lesions of so-called association areas that produce apraxias and agnosias.

Apraxia is often defined as an inability to perform purposeful movements not accompanied by sensory loss or paralysis. It is a manifestation of a cerebral lesion. But the organism with spinal transection withdraws from a noxious stimulus—a purposeful movement—so the organism is not paralyzed in the sense of having no ability to move a member. Total inability to move occurs with very low-level lesions such as extensive section of ventral (motor) roots. All paralysis occasioned by central nervous system lesions can be viewed as varying degrees of apraxia ranging from the least severe, in which there is no response to abstract stimuli, to the most severe, in which there is no response to very concrete stimuli. A striking example of stimulus hierarchy and adequacy to evoke a response appears in cases of apraxia of lips and tongue. Asked to "show me how you blow out a match," a patient whose language function and understanding are intact does not respond. Hold up nothing between thumb and forefinger and ask the patient to "blow out this match," and still no response occurs. Hold up an unlighted match, and command, "blow this out"—and a distorted, poorly directed puff may come out of the side of the mouth; but hold up a lighted match near the face, and it is swiftly, unerringly blown out.

The continuum from concrete to abstract includes the "as if" phenomenon at its abstract end. When we request the apraxic patient to wave goodbye (which often cannot be done), we are really saying behave *as if* someone were leaving. In the concrete situation of a friend leaving, the apraxic patient can wave goodbye; but in the *as if* situation, it cannot be done. "Show me how you brush your teeth" means, "behave *as if* you had a toothbrush." The level of response declines according to the severity of the lesion, from the abstract performance with nothing in hand to the more concrete performance of doing it with a finger to the most concrete performance of doing it with a toothbrush.

The *as if* phenomenon appears in children's puzzles, which often constitute a measure of maturation of the nervous system. The familiar Fork in the Road puzzle exemplifies this: two Indian tribes live in the region of a fork in the road. Members of one tribe always tell the truth. Members of the other tribe always lie. An Indian—tribe unspecified—stands at the fork in the road. Puzzle question: What one question can you ask to put you on the correct road to Tucscon? What has always interested me about puzzles like this is that normal adults divide into two categories: those who can and those who cannot solve the riddle. Of those who cannot, there are two categories: those who can understand the explanation and those who cannot. This demonstrates at least three levels of comprehension in the normal (as determined by social standards) nervous system of the *as if* level of performance—that is, three levels of ability to appreciate an abstract stimulus.[1]

On the input side, the high-level disorder is called agnosia, a dictionary definition of which is an inability to recognize objects by use of the senses. This is as unsatisfactory as defining paralysis as an inability to move. Input to the sensory side is also graded from the most concrete (or biologically significant) to the most abstract. A patient with visual agnosia may not be able to demonstrate how to drink using a partially closed fist as a surrogate for a glass and may not be able to demonstrate it with an empty glass—or even a full one; but leave the full glass on the bedside table, and, when thirsty, the patient will casually and naturally lift it and drink. This patient, who cannot "see," can walk through doorways and down staircases. Agnosia is not only a pathological state, for it also occurs in the normal. We simply do not recognize it as abnormal when we encounter it in everyday life. In grade school, the student group was divided into "singers" and "listeners," for there were some who could not carry a tune, being "tone deaf"—the analogue, in normal subjects, of pathologic "psychic blindness." Some tone deaf know they cannot carry a tone. Others believe they are on pitch, having agnosia for their agnosia. Think of the scene from bygone Americana—(visualize a *Saturday Evening Post* cover) that of the jolly butcher boy cheerfully whistling as he makes his delivery, enjoying himself because he doesn't know he is off key. Nervous systems differ.

Agnosia is not only a pathological state, for it also occurs in the normal.

What makes these entities of interest in an analysis of conscious awareness is that, at one level, the percept is intact—the thirsty patient drinks. At another level, that percept—the conscious awareness indicated—is no longer an effective stimulus. But the awareness of it has already been indicated. Is it the consciousness component of that percept that is impaired? Such circumscribed affection of consciousness is dealt with by passing it off as inattention.

If the clinical loss of consciousness secondary to diffuse cerebral or brain stem injuries represents the negative of brain stem reticular formation–generated "readiness" (not to be confused with the readiness potential of the electroencephalogram), and if apraxia and agnosia represent the negative of conscious awareness, what then is the negative of self-consciousness—the awareness of awareness? Two entities come to mind, the first of which is perhaps suspect. There is a disorder called Anton's syndrome which, if it exists, is described as cortical blindness accompanied by denial of blindness.[2] If the cortical blindness—that is, visual agnosia—is construed as a loss of conscious awareness of the visual experience, then the denial of blindness (a denial of absent conscious awareness becomes an agnosia for an agnosia, or an absent awareness of an absent awareness—in other words, absent self-consciousness. The more familiar form of negative self-consciousness is termed anosognosia—a denial of abnormality. This is often seen in right parietal lesions in which inattention to left space occurs. This inattention applies to personal as well as extrapersonal space, so the left arm is often unattended. It may hang awkwardly out of bed or remain useless (if it is recognized—for it is often not recognized by its owner as a part of his or her body) in activities in which it would ordinarily be used. Not only is the arm employed defectively or not used at all, but if the disorder is pointed out, the patient will deny there is anything amiss. Often anosognosia is seen in conjunction with autotopagnosia—the lack of recognition of a body part. Autotopagnosia and the associated anosognosia—the denial of abnormality of the unrecognized body part—demonstrate the unawareness of unawareness in personal space that Anton's syndrome demonstrates in extrapersonal space.

15

Buy One, Get One Free: Volition

Any discussion of consciousness must confront the issue of volition—conscious will—fraught as it is with philosophic baggage. Volition is defined by the dictionary as the faculty of conscious will—and especially of deliberate action. The inclusion of action in the definition emphasizes the role of movement. Movement as produced by the nervous system has been divided traditionally into two major categories: voluntary and involuntary. Until recently, voluntary movement was ascribed to the cortical (so-called pyramidal) system and involuntary movement to the extra-pyramidal system—in particular to the cerebellum. Previous discussion has indicated that input other than volition can release cortical action, and studies on the cerebellum in the past several decades indicate a much wider field of effect than just upon involuntary movement.

Thomas Willis (for whom the arterial Circle of Willis at the base of the brain is named) studied the brain during the seventeenth-century resurgence of interest in human anatomy. He did this in a society permeated with the teachings of St. Thomas Aquinas and an overwhelming concept of sin—the era of Cromwell and the Puritans. Aquinas (1225 (?)–1274), "the angelic doctor" had analyzed the seven mortal, or deadly, sins in

Summa Theologiae and *On Evil*, and his teachings resurfaced during Willis's era.

Sin comes in two varieties. Venial sins are transgressions committed without the full consent of the will, or full awareness of their seriousness. Involuntary sins do not deprive the soul of divine grace—unlike mortal sins, serious transgressions that are willfully committed. In this intellectual climate, Willis examined the brain and saw a big brain—the cerebrum—above, and a small brain—he called it the cerebell—below. He pondered the purposes of these two brains and concluded that the large one related to voluntary (mortal) action and the small one to involuntary (venial) action. This formulation set the stage for conceptualization of the voluntary and involuntary functions of the motor components of the nervous system for the next three hundred years.

The "voluntary" motor cortex of the cerebrum is characterized anatomically by giant pyramidal nerve cells in its fifth layer. From these emerge the fibers that conduct the impulses that ultimately descend to the spinal cord for motor performance. To these giant pyramidal cells was ascribed the function of voluntary movement. Until recently it was thought these cells generated the impulses directly responsible for the ultimate innervation of muscle. Then, by microelectrode studies on single cells in cortexes of conscious monkeys, it was shown that pyramidal tract neurons fire immediately before instrumental performance in a conditioned act and cease firing as the movement is initiated. These cells anticipate the movement. Anticipatory firing has also been observed in posterior parietal cortex, which, from layer five, sends fibers to the spinal cord. This activity in advance of the motor performance can be construed as a manifestation or neural counterpart of conscious will.

In the intact human an analog is found in the readiness potential recorded electroencephalographically in central regions (the region of motor cortex), or in the electroencephalographic finding called contingent negative variation. In each a buildup of negative potential is recorded in the few seconds preceding motor performance. Contingent negative variation employs a warning signal and an imperative signal to initiate the act. (On your mark . . . go!). Between the two a slow negative potential appears that disappears with the imperative signal. The readiness potential is a similar buildup of a slow negative potential (depending on the predictability and probability of the motor act) but can be either self-paced or in response to an expected stimulus. Because of the geometry of recording with surface electrodes, what appears as a discrete spike with a microelectrode may appear at the surface as a slow negative potential when generated by a group of cells. These electrical changes signal the voluntary aspect of the subsequent motor act and are the electrophysiological analogue of conscious will. Consciousness of the act is thought to be delayed by at least 350 milliseconds following the onset of neural activity. That is, neuronal activity precedes the "volition," which, in turn, precedes the action. According to this formulation, consciousness is equated with awareness. It is awareness of the intended act—the wish—that is delayed. Delay is also true of sensation, of which one is not aware until about half a second after stimulation. Is this not really a restatement of the subliminal experience: that a stimulus must have a minimal duration to reach awareness (minimal stimulus duration and awareness delay are not equal) but may have an effect (behavioral or electrographic) before that duration—that is, it is subliminal with respect to awareness? Once again, this displays the existence of consciousness without awareness, because, in the subliminal phase, something is happening. It is as if every experience (perceptual or action) is preceded by a subliminal prologue before achieving awareness. The subliminal prologue may be for neural registration of stimulus or of response. Accordingly, the minimal stimulus duration or interval (a physical event) required to achieve perception is of different duration from the delay of awareness (a psychophysical event). Muscle serves as a good model by which to distinguish the physical event from the physiologic. If the interstimulus interval is reduced serially, the indirectly stimulated muscle responses show a similar decline in inter-response interval, up to a certain point. Further reduction of inter-stimulus interval, which continues to evoke dual responses, is not accompanied by further reduction of inter-response interval. To continue the analogy with muscle, an end-plate potential (subliminal) of

Volition is signaled prior to action and disappears at the onset of performance

sufficient voltage initiates a spike (volition), which initiates a contraction (action). In this analogy, the electromechanical coupling of muscle represents the expression of will in behavior.

Thus volition is signaled prior to action and disappears at the onset of performance. In this way, voluntary action—or volition—introduces into consciousness the third epoch. Consciousness of the past is recorded in conscious memory, a conceptual state for which the immediate stimulus is internal—within the nervous system. Consciousness of the present is inscribed in conscious awareness as a perceptual experience, for which the immediate stimulus is external—in one of the three environments. Consciousness of the future is indicated by the preparatory potentials of volition, for which the immediate stimulus may be internal, external, or both. Is it coincidence that the noun *will*, denoting volition—as in conscious will—is also the verb *will*, signifying future intent—as in "I will go"?

16

Play It Again: Speculative Reprise

Evolution has left its mark on the nervous system. Early-evolved, low levels of function are modified by the serial addition of higher levels of structure and function, the alterations of behavior a result of the modification—often inhibition—introduced by these higher levels. But the low-level function is always present, available for release when control by higher regions is removed. The nervous system, because of evolutionary acquisitions, is hierarchically organized with recursion of processes, a general principle of organization.

Somewhere in evolution, consciousness arises. Like other functions, it is hierarchically organized, develops out of preexisting structures, and is elaborated by imposition of functions from above; it reaches its greatest development in the form of self-consciousness. At all levels it operates in parallel with other systems. This parallel operation does not preclude it being part of, and developed in, these other systems.

Parallel processing is a recurrent theme in the nervous system. The hierarchical organization of a given system suggests that individual systems are organized in series. But these serially organized systems can operate in parallel—one with another. Often an early-evolved system functions simultaneous with a later-evolved one. Autonomic activity is constant, ongoing, and parallel with the serial function of cerebral systems. Affective coloring is given to sensations and percepts by the limbic system—an early cortical endowment—in parallel with the perceptual experience. Consciousness, too, operates in parallel with other systems, even though it may be created in part by those systems.

Three concentric spheres of environment are monitored by three concentric tubes of the nervous system. The innermost environment—the viscera—is controlled by the innermost layer of nerve cells—the intermediolateral horn cells, the periventricular gray of the brain stem, the hypothalamus, and the orbitofrontal cortex. The middle environment of the body wall is transduced by proprioceptors, including vestibular, and is conveyed to the middle gray layer of the nervous system, the subcortical nuclei. The external environmental sphere of the world around us is reported to the late-developed outer neuronal layer of cerebral cortex.

The function of the nervous system as a totality is to model reality—the reality of the three environments. How that reality is represented is not known, but it is certainly not biologically isomorphic. The modeling of the environment is an active process in which the nervous system operates on the environment even as the environment operates on the nervous system. This operation occurs at any given perceptual moment but also occurs longitudinally over time. The history of experience is reflected in morphology, particularly at early developmental stages of the individual—so-called critical periods. Experience thus tunes the nervous system and sculpts subsequence experience.

The function of the nervous system as a totality is to model reality

Experience also shapes physiologic function, sometimes by way of structural change. A frequently used network develops new synapses and new dendritic spines. A practiced act is more easily performed than a new one. A nerve cell that has fired may easily fire again. A synapse that is frequently used may exhibit long-term potentiation.

Information from the environments is conducted centrally by specific and by nonspecific systems. The specific systems are organized into tracts and lemnisci, nuclear aggregates and cortical areas. Each specific system is modality marked and carries information only about its specific modality. The nonspecific systems are diffuse in projection, reticulate in termination, and modality nonspecific. Collateral input from the specific to the nonspecific systems loses its modality identification. Input to the reticular formation from one sensory system has the same effect as input from any other sensory system. From the brain stem this nonspecific reticular system projects down to the spinal cord and up to cortex. It facilitates function and, in the case of the ascending reticular activating system, constitutes the first instantiation of cortical consciousness.

This system, which activates or arouses the cerebrum, functions tonically, produces various levels of arousal and is continuously active. The sleeping individual is ready to receive and react to stimuli—in other words, is conscious. In its rostral projection, this consciousness system becomes attached to sensory and perceptual inputs—among others— and is shaped by higher-level modification into conscious awareness. Input recursion amplifies consciousness readiness to produce conscious awareness.[1] The awareness system requires the presence of a stimulus such as a percept, which can then serve in its turn as a stimulus to project to higher conceptual levels, where the remodeling produces awareness of awareness, consciousness of consciousness, or consciousness of itself—called self-consciousness. Thus consciousness is a layered process, not a unitary entity; in this aspect it mimics the organization of other neurological systems, such as the sensory or motor systems.

Consciousness is a threshold phenomenon. A threshold is demonstrated by the emergence from an assembly of identical modules of a property that does not inhere within an individual module. The module for consciousness has not been identified. Consideration should be given to the possibility that the cortical column is the module for conscious awareness. A column in a network of one configuration would, by way of its specific input, participate in a generation of a percept. In a second assembly, its nonspecific input would participate in the genesis of cortical consciousness. The modular column would have a dual role, accounting for the tight linkage between consciousness and awareness of the percept.

Organization of a hierarchical system can be explored by examining the loss or release of function caused by a lesion. Care must be taken to distinguish the negative from the positive effects of the lesion. The negative effect—the absence of function—gives information about processes at the level of the lesion. The positive effect—movement or sensation— displays a phenomenon, produced at a lower level, that has been released by the lesion. Destruction of the lowest level ablates the function entirely—all movement is lost in spinal destruction. Lesions at higher levels destroy the modifications of the coarse fundament of behavior represented at low levels. If the consciousness system is hierarchically organized, lesions should be able not only to impair basic representation but nullify the modifications located at higher levels.

An injury to the brain stem—analogous to loss of all movement in the case of spinal destruction—may cause complete loss of cortical consciousness. Autonomic and low-level reflex activity persist, but other functions are abolished. The organism is unable to respond to stimuli at a cortical level. Lesions of primary cortical projection areas (or of subcortical pathways to these areas) in the presence of intact brain stem function abolish conscious awareness of the percept that would be focally represented in the cortical region were it intact. General consciousness is not affected, because the distribution of the nonspecific input is widespread. The circumscribed loss of conscious awareness of the percept that would otherwise be represented in the intact cortical area can be ascribed to inability to construct the percept because of damage to the specific modality-marked input—or it can be ascribed to a circumscribed abnormality of consciousness mediated by the nonspecific system. Evidence for this is obtained by the method of double simultaneous stimulation, which demonstrates that the percept can be appreciated if delivered singly, or its spatial or temporal extent increased when delivered simultaneously with the contralateral stimulus. Thus perception of the stimulus (at least in that context) is intact. Circumscribed loss of conscious awareness in the presence of intact perception may relate to the presumed tight linkage of specific and nonspecific systems at the individual module. The separation of percept from conscious awareness of it may be a function of the architecture of the assembly rather than of the single module—in other words, a different network existing for the specific and nonspecific components of a percept.

Lateralized inattention demonstrated by double simultaneous stimulation is limited to one field (one lateral half of space) in contrast to consciousness as generally considered, which is a bilateral phenomenon. This should not be construed to mean that consciousness is a dominant function in the sense that a unilateral focal lesion can produce a global defect that crosses the midline. Rather, it indicates that the cortical neural activity supporting consciousness is widespread and generalized. Whether a single unilateral focal lesion can produce a bilateral alteration of the state (level) of consciousness cannot be explored satisfactorily because of the association of other dominant functions located in the region of damage, the affection of which contaminates the examination of consciousness.[2]

The phenomena of anosognosia and autotopagnosia approach the question of dominance with respect to self-consciousness. Self-consciousness—consciousness of consciousness—is the highest level in the consciousness hierarchy. That dominance and self-consciousness can be related is not surprising when one recalls that dominance is always related to high-level function. Denial of abnormality of an affected limb of which one is unaware—a lack of consciousness of a lack of consciousness—is a loss of self-consciousness in an isolated sphere. However, the patient with a right parietal lesion denies abnormality of the left arm (which may not be recognized by the owner as the owners') whether it is presented in the left or in the right visual field. The defect of recognition—the denial of abnormality—the loss of self-consciousness in this circumscribed arena—crosses the midline and is a bilateral defect produced by a unilateral lesion.

To view it from the other side, a lesion of dominant hemisphere can produce a constellation of signs known as Gerstmann's syndrome. Thought by some to be a component, or partial expression, of aphasia, it consists of agraphia (inability to write), acalculia (inability to calculate), right–left confusion and finger agnosia. The inability to identify fingers is for both hands in either field of vision—that is, the left hand in the right and left fields of vision, and the same for the right hand. A unilateral injury produces bilateral autotopagnosia for fingers, unless this is con-strued simply as a naming disorder that is part of aphasia.

Even if dominance for a circumscribed aspect of consciousness could be established, this would not diminish the force of the argument that at a cortical level, consciousness is widely distributed, may be partially lat-eralized (as in inattention), and has a widespread anatomic base.

The emphasis thus far has been spatial. But time also must be considered—even if only in a speculative way. Suppose—just suppose—that the organisms from which we evolved (reptiles, say—or, better still, amphibia) have no neural mechanism sufficiently elaborated to allow awareness (never mind self-consciousness). And suppose—just suppose—that stimuli in humans traverse the "lower" (phylogenetically older) neu-ral pathways first, later reaching the more evolved regions of the central nervous system. A conceivable outcome could be that a peripheral stim-ulus recapitulates in its spatial course (therefore time) of transmission some of the evolutionary stages that culminated in the elaboration of a forebrain composed of multiple assemblies of neurological modules associated with the genesis of conscious awareness. The early millisec-onds of transmission—in the spinal cord and the brain stem—would occur without consciousness. Events at this stage would be uncon-scious, nonconscious, or preconscious but would constitute the sub-strate for the emergent property of "readiness," activation, or arousal of the still-to-be-developed (evolved) cerebral hemispheres. Subsequent milliseconds of transmission, with arrival at the thalamus and primary projection areas, would engender awareness and its associated qualia of limbic affective overlay. Only the late milliseconds of transmission would affect the late-acquired cortical areas, whose assemblies underlie awareness of awareness. This dynamic, allegorical evolutionary recapitulation in time (the analogue of the allegorical, evolutionary recapitulation of the human nervous system in space, its parts developing from the oldest to the most recent) would help us understand some of the problems raised by such things as early- and late-event-related cortical potentials, readiness potential and contingent negative variation, and "automatic" movements and procedural memory. If this view has any value, it might also help explain why "for inclusion in the conscious field a neuronal assembly has to attain and hold a critical level of activation for a critical period of time."[3]

If one accepts the notion that a critical amount of forebrain is necessary for conscious awareness and agrees that creatures much lower on the phylogenetic scale—creatures without a significant amount of forebrain—behave (that is, move in response to a stimulus), the question of whether consciousness (in the transitive sense) is necessary for behavior answers itself—unless, of course, behavior is redefined to imply awareness, intent, or intentionality. But intent and intentionality, in contrast to awareness, do not, as usually defined, imply the need for a forebrain. Pockett's abstract plans for movement,[4] Freeman's "endogenous initiation, construction, and direction of behavior into the world,"[5] and Pacherie's division of intentions into initiating function, sustaining function, and monitoring function[6] are not incompatible with what is usually called reflex behavior (stimulus-response without awareness) and do not imply the need for a conscious forebrain. Even awareness does not require a forebrain. Reflex behavior, generally considered to occur without awareness, must, in some sense, imply awareness even if the responding organism is not aware of the awareness. Reflex behavior is a stimulus-response product. Stimulus is defined by response, response is defined by neural activity that evokes goal-directed behavior (even if only withdrawal)—so intent and awareness must be present. In this sense the question of employing behavior as a criterion (as an operational definition) of awareness must be answered in the affirmative without the implication of awareness of awareness. The intent of reflex behavior is immediate—what Pacherie identifies as present directed (as contrasted with future directed)[7] or Mele terms proximal (as contrasted with distal) intentions.[8] Pacherie's motor intentions—her third category, which "neuroscientists call motor representations"[9] are, of course, immediate, and they participate in the stimulus–response reflex. It is only when you accept Malle's proposal that "intentions . . . are the output of a reasoning process"[10] that stimulus–response reflex behavior is excluded. The development in evolutionary time of behavior—responses to stimuli—prior to the advent of forebrain-associated awareness is reflected in transmission time of neural activity to the forebrain, the early phases of which transmission are without awareness.[11]

17

In the End: Conclusion

Consciousness is manifestation of brain function. It is the result of a process generated by the nonspecific components of the nervous system. Like other neurological functions, it is hierarchically organized and represented at multiple levels in the nervous system. It is generated by spinal and brain stem input to the ascending reticular activating system, from which it is projected to subcortical nuclei and cortex, where it is widely displayed. It is a phenomenon shared with other animals but is most developed in human beings.

Consciousness is a threshold phenomenon, an entity produced by an assembly of identical modules that does not inhere within any individual module. The high-level organization of the assembly may include the cortical column as the module. If included, the cortical column, which receives specific and nonspecific input, can then participate in two separate assemblies, one of which generates perceptual experience and the second of which generates consciousness of that experience, or conscious awareness. This postulate helps understand the tight linkage that exists in conscious awareness between percept and awareness. At higher levels of elaboration, awareness of awareness is represented. This consciousness of consciousness is termed self-consciousness.

Because consciousness is hierarchically organized, it can be interrupted at several levels by pathological processes. Loss of consciousness can be generalized when the generator in the brain stem is affected. It can be generalized when the termination in cortex is widely damaged. It can be focally impaired when a cortical sector is injured. Because the focal impairment exists on a background of intact function, it may be hard to appreciate. Focal impairment of conscious awareness exists when a percept appreciated under one set of circumstances cannot be appreciated in another. This occurs in the absence of structural injury when the temporal or spatial aspects of a stimulus are reduced below a critical level. In these circumstances the disorder is apparently not one of perception but of consciousness of the perception. Such disorder can be limited to the function represented in an injured neural sector. Lack of recognition of the lack of recognition occurs with lesions of the next higher (perhaps the highest) level. This agnosia for an agnosia—as seen in anosognosia with autotopagnosia—can be viewed as a loss of a sector of self-consciousness.

Finally, as demonstrated by memory and volition, consciousness operating in the present can operate on the past or on the future.

What it comes down to is this: the term consciousness appears in at least two senses, which have not always been kept separate. One, the intransitive sense, is the state of readiness to respond. Two, the transitive sense, is consciousness of, and requires, an object of which to be aware. Accordingly, the term awareness is often used interchangeably with the transitive form of consciousness. A problem arises when it is shown that awareness can exist in the normal human, and in pathological brain states in the human, without awareness of it. Response to subliminal stimuli, electrographic changes, "blindsight," alteration of galvanic skin resistance, pupillary constriction to retinal illumination, and starting to run before hearing the starting gun all demonstrate awareness without awareness of awareness—or consciousness of without consciousness of consciousness of.

What we are talking about when we talk of human consciousness is really awareness of awareness, consciousness of consciousness—self-consciousness. Other animals have consciousness (transitive), as indicated by their object awareness and goal-directed behavior. What we do not know is whether they are aware of their awareness, whether they have self-consciousness, or whether self-consciousness is a uniquely human characteristic. Just as recursion is an underlying principle of neurological organization, reflected in language, so, too, is consciousness reflected in humans' self-consciousness of which they are conscious—an infinite regression.

Appendix

The Cool Web

Children are dumb to say how hot the day is,
How hot the scent is of the summer rose,
How dreadful the black wastes of evening sky,
How dreadful the tall soldiers drumming by.

But we have speech, to chill the angry day,
And speech, to dull the rose's cruel scent.
We spell away the overhanging night,
We spell away the soldiers and the fright.

There's a cool web of language winds us in,
Retreat from too much joy or too much fear:
We grow sea-green at last and coldly die
In brininess and volubility.

But if we let our tongues lose self-possession,
Throwing off language and its watery clasp
Before our death, instead of when death comes,
Facing the wide glare of the children's day,
Facing the rose, the dark sky and the drums,
We shall go mad no doubt and die that way.

—Robert Graves, 1927

Notes

Chapter 1 In the Begninning: Introduction

1. Donoghue, D. "The Pragmatic American," *Harper's Magazine* 315 (January 2007):90.

Chapter 2 This I Believe: Preview

1. Honderich 2004, 203.
2. Pacherie, in Pockett 2006, 160.
3. Institute for Systems Biology website.
4. Searle 2004, 149.
5. Honderich 2004, 218.
6. Chalmers 1996, 125.
7. Chalmers 1996, 127.
8. Humphrey 2006, 137.
9. Searle 2004, 139.
10. Honderich 2004, 97.
11. Searle 2004, 139.
12. Steriad, in Kryger et al. 1989, 111.
13. Steriad, in Kryger et al. 1989, 112.
14. Crick 1994.
15. Hebb 1949, xix.
16. Passingham and Lau, in Pockett 2006, 65.

Chapter 3 This They Believe: Other Views

1. Libet 2004, 203.
2. Crick 1994, 248–249.
3. Crick 1994, 267.
4. Pockett et al. 2006, 13.
5. Crick 1994, 267.
6. In addition to Pockett's "externally produced touch" (p. 42) and Crick's "free will" (p. 267) a hasty review of "The New Cognitive Neurosciences" discloses 16 other functions "located" in the anterior cingulate.
7. Pockett et al. 2006, 22.
8. Koch 2004, 34.
9. Koch 2004, 286.
10. Koch 2004, 293 (italics added).
11. Koch 2004, 294.
12. Koch 2004, 301.
13. Searle *NYRB* 42: No. 17 and 18. November 2 and 16, 1995.
14. Chalmers *NYRB* 44: No. 8. May 15, 1997.
15. Chalmers 1996, 234.
16. Chalmers, *Ibid.*
17. Searle *NYRB* 44: No. 8. May 15, 1997.
18. Crick 1994, 21.
19. Koch 2004, 2.
20. Honderich 2004, 132.
21. Searle 2004, 84.
22. Searle, *NYRB* 52: No. 1. January 13, 2005.
23. Searle, *Ibid*, 37.
24. Koch 2004, 88.
25. Koch 2004, 87.
26. Koch 2004, 16.
27. Koch 2004, 88.
28. Koch 2004, 93.
29. Koch 2004, 320.
30. Searle *NYRB* 52, No. 1, 37: January 13, 2005.
31. Koch 2004, 93.
32. *Ibid.*
33. A captious question—really quite minor in the context of our subject. Do patients with Parkinson's disease, Alzheimer's disease, and other forms of dementia have disturbances of consciousness, or do they only have dementia—a decline from a former intellectual level? Dementia is an alteration of cognition. Cognition is related to conceptualization. Conceptualization is an outgrowth of perception and sensation. It can be impaired prior to, and without concomitant impairment of, perception or sensation. Accepting (for the moment) the Crick-Koch equation of consciousness with awareness (or percepts), does this mean that with cognitive decline, consciousness is impaired? Consider this in light of the statement (p. 302) "That many aspects of high-level cognition, such as decision making, planning and creativity are beyond the pale of awareness." p. 91 in Koch makes me wonder; see also p. 130 and the "fully conscious" drug-induced late-stage Parkinson patient.
34. Hobson 1999, 67.
35. Hobson (Ibid., 68).

36. Chalmers 1996, 11.
37. *Ibid*.
38. Chalmers 1996, 28.
39. *Ibid*.
40. Chalmers 1996, 11.
41. Damasio, in Metzinger 2000, 119.
42. *Ibid*.
43. *Ibid*.
44. Damasio, in Metzinger 2000, 117.
45. Damasio, in Metzinger 2000, 115.
46. *Ibid*.
47. Damasio, in Metzinger 2000, 112.
48. Damasio, in Metzinger 2000, 119.
49. Libet 2004, 67.
50. Steriade, in Kryger et al. 1989, 115.
51. Libet 2004, 59.
52. Libet 2004, 50.
53. Passingham and Lau, in Pockett 2006, 54.
54. Libet 2004, 168.
55. Libet 2004, 179.
56. Libet 2005, 179–180.
57. Libet 2004, 182.
58. Functional magnetic resonance imaging and positron emission tomography actually measure blood flow. The assumption that blood flow correlates with neuronal activity is probably justified, but the assumption that the blood flow is proportional to impulse activity may not be. Active blood flow may represent an increase of spike-generation, but it may also occur with a decrease. It also relates to synaptic activity and metabolic needs independent of spike genesis, and, if the neuronal activity is inhibitory, blood flow may increase while function declines.
59. Passingham and Lau, in Pockett 2006, 68.
60. Dennett 1996, 64.
61. *Ibid*.
62. Searle, *NYRB* 52, 36.
63. Morgan 1995, 105.
64. Hobson 1999, 97.
65. Hobson 1999, 99.
66. Bourgeois, in Gazzaniga 2000, 49.
67. Bourgeois, in Gazzaniga 2000, 50.
68. Stein, in Gazzaniga 2000, 68.
69. Stein, Figure 5.5, in Gazzaniga 2000, 62.
70. Choudhury and Blakemore, in Pockett 2006, 49.
71. *Annual Review of Neuroscience*, 2004: 27, 167–192.
72. Hurley, in Pockett 2006, 312.
73. Hurley, in Pockett 2006, 313.
74. Dennett 1996, 20.
75. *Ibid*.
76. *Ibid*.
77. Dennett 1996, 21.
78. McKeon 1941, 564.
79. Chalmers, in Metzinger 2000, 19.
80. Chalmers, in Metzinger 2000, 22.

81. Chalmers, in Metzinger 2000, 23.
82. Chalmers, in Metzinger 2000, 33.
83. Edelman 2004, 9–10.
84. Hobson 1999, 198.
85. Edelman 2004, 122.
86. Flohr, in Metzinger 2000, 250.
87. *Ibid.*
88. DeHaene, Changeut, Naccache, Sergent, *Trends in Cognitive Sciences* 2006, 204.
89. *Ibid.*
90. Searle 2004, 151.
91. Searle 2004, 155.
92. Searle *NYRB* 52, 36.
93. Koch 2004, 296.
94. Humphrey 2006, 13.
95. Humphrey 2006, 14.
96. Edelman 2004, 10.
97. Edelman 2004, 62.
98. Once again the clinic offers special insights unavailable elsewhere. Post-encephalitic Parkinsonism, a sequel of viral encephalitis, is characterized by the occurrence (among other manifestations) of oculogyric crises. These episodes, which occur erratically, consist of the eyes being driven into a fixed position of gaze and compulsively maintained there. That it is a compulsion can be demonstrated by exhorting (a euphemism for shouting) the patient to change the position of the eyes. "Look at me!" you shout at the patient during a spell and the eyes leave the fixed posture to look at you. "Very good" you say and the eyes immediately return to the original fixed position. The compulsion is frequently accompanied by an obsessive thought that goes round and round until the crisis is over. Patients are often reluctant to talk about this but, on occasion, will.

Many years ago I was meeting with a group of Neurology Residents in the Department Library. They told me of a patient with post-encephalitic Parkinsonism and then had him join us in the Library. We explored the issue of obsessive thoughts during a crisis. "When your eyes are driven to the side do you have a recurrent thought?" I asked (the quotes are reconstructions). "Yes," he said. "What is the thought?" I asked. "I'm looking at the books, I'm looking at the books," he said, indicating the bookshelves to his left—the direction in which his eyes were usually driven. "What if you were sitting where I am?" I asked—a position that would put the bookshelves on his right. "What would you think then?" "I'm looking at the window, I'm looking at the window," he replied. "So it's always different?" I asked. "Yes," he said; "it's always different—but it's always the same."

Complicated? Of course. But I understood it to mean that the percept was always different depending upon where he was and what his eyes saw during the crisis. But the feeling—the emotional accompaniment, the quale—was always the same.

It takes a pathological disorder in which one component of a twinned pair is destroyed (as in a stroke for example) or overactive (as in a seizure or oculogyric crisis) to display one member of the pair in isolation or in sharp contrast to the other.
99. Chalmers 1996, 359.
100. Chalmers 1996, 4.

101. Chalmers 1996, 359.
102. Honderich 2004, 110.
103. Honderich 2004, 122.
104. Honderich 2004, 132.
105. Searle 2004, 84.
106. Searle, *NYRB* 42. Numbers 17 and 18, November 2, 1995, and November 16, 1995.
107. Edelman 2004, 10.
108. Edelman 2004, 3.
109. Humphrey 2006, 49–50.
110. Edelman 2004, 65.
111. Searle 2004, 118 .
112. Humphrey 2006, 15.
113. Laming, Oxford Companion to the Mind: 1987, 657.
114. Searle, *NYRB* 52: 42, No. 1, November 2, 1995.
115. *Ibid.*
116. Edelman 2004, 64.
117. Edelman 2004, 70.
118. Edelman 2004, 64.
119. Humphrey 2006, 19–21.
120. Pockett 2006, 11 in Pockett et al.
121. Freeman 2006, 76 in Pockett et al.
122. Searle 2004, 28.
123. Banks, 250 in Pockett 2006.
124. Dennet 1996, 35.
125. Edelman 2004, 125.
126. *Ibid.*
127. *Ibid.*
128. Searle 2004, 139.
129. Dennet 1996, 36.
130. Dennet 1996, 35.
131. Honderich 2004, 177.
132. Humphrey 2006, 92.
133. Chalmers 1996, 22.
134. Honderich 2004, 169.
135. Locke 1977, p. 72 in Sagass, Gershon, and Friedhoff.
136. Humphrey 2006, 90.
137. Chalmers 1996, 107.
138. Chalmers 1996, 128.
139. *Ibid.*
140. Chalmers 1996, 129.
141. Kinsbourne 2006, *Cortex* 42, 869–874.
142. Edelman 2004, 7.
143. Libet 2004, 190.
144. Singer, in Metzinger 2000, 123.
145. *Ibid.*
146. Singer, in Metzinger 2000, 124.
147. Singer, in Metzinger 2000, 134.
148. Crick 1994.
149. Searle 2004, 136–137.

150. Honderich 2004, 46.
151. Honderich 2004, 20.
152. Honderich 2004, 21.
153. *Ibid.*
154. Honderich 2004, 37.
155. Searle 2004, 150.
156. Honderich 2004, 68.
157. Honderich 2004, 98.
158. Honderich 2004, 104.
159. Hobson 1999, 16.
160. Honderich 2004, 105.
161. Honderich 2004, 107.
162. Honderich 2004, 108.
163. Honderich 2004, 20.
164. Honderich 2004, 109.
165. Honderich 2004, 133.
166. Honderich 2004, 155.
167. Honderich 2004, 156.
168. Honderich 2004, 178.
169. Edelman 2004, 10.
170. Here are some brief case reports that make me question the validity of hallucinations in the strict sense of the term:

 a. A young schizophrenic, E. M. (you will have to guess her last name), kept repeating to herself "the Golden Arches." How easy it would have been to infer she was seeing something not there. She often said she heard voices projected from a laundry outside of the hospital where her father was employed. Working late one night in my quiet hospital office I heard voices (unintelligible) coming out of the heating duct. Our ward, labs, and offices were on the top floor of the building so the voices must have been coming from below. In the basement of our building was the hospital laundry with its noisy night crew.

 b. A distinguished gentleman was admitted to a private hospital for alcoholism. On occasion, following a binge, he would experience delirium tremens, about which he freely talked. During the DTs, he sometimes had visual hallucinations. When I asked him to describe them he pointed to the window—a sash that had hook-like handles attached to the bottom of the frame. "To give you an example" he said "I look at that handle. It starts to shimmer, then it moves from side to side, then it becomes a rat's head sticking out of the wall and I get scared" (quotes are reconstructed).

 c. A colleague and I were stopped outside the open door of a room that belonged to a patient with acute anuria and uremic encephalopathy—a disorder in which seizures may occur. We were discussing the wisdom of starting prophylactic use of an anticonvulsant called Dilantin. When we went to see him he was thrashing about and calling out "the lantern, the lantern." How easy it would have been to conclude he was having visual hallucinations.

 d. A young Greek man with a primary brain tumor (glioblastoma multiforme) in temporal lobe had seizures in which he "heard music." When asked what music he said it was either Tchaikovsky or a Greek folk tune, he couldn't tell which (not one on one occasion, the other on another occasion; rather when he heard it he didn't know which it was). This internally generated auditory hallucination was not a well-formed percept.

e. An elderly woman who lived alone with her dog suffered a stroke causing a left homonymous hemianopia ("blindness" in the left visual field). As she began to recover she experienced twinkling in the lower half of the field much as we experience pins and needles in a limb recovering from having "fallen asleep." She described this as a vision of her dog. She knew it was not real, a so-called pseudo-hallucination. When asked to describe it she would say, "I see my dog." "What does it look like?" I would ask. "My dog?" she replied. He is brown and white . . ." "No," I would say. "What you see. What does it look like?" "It looks like my dog." "Describe it" I would request. "My dog is brown and white . . ." And so on. What she saw, I suspect, was apparent movement in the recovering field; to this woman, movement at ground level meant her dog. Her nervous system operated on this input (we all do it all the time) to create something not in the stimulus, to make it a "dog"—a hallucination, but she did not describe the hallucination (only her dog) because it was not a well-formed percept (quotes are reconstructed).

f. A former alcoholic suffered post-traumatic temporal lobe epilepsy as the result of a head injury he had sustained while drinking. Each seizure included a sense of intense activity at the extreme periphery of his right visual field. He described the activity as a lot of very little people in colorful hats who were dancing or jumping but he could never see them clearly, for when he turned to bring them into focus they promptly moved away. "If I am going to see things," he said "I might as well be drinking."

171. Edelman 2004, 7.

172. Koch 2004, 270.

173. Searle 2004, 137.

174. Honderich 2004, 105.

175. Honderich 2004, 174.

176. "The periphery is the real lowest level but we shall speak of three levels of central evolution." The lowest central level "represents all parts of the body most nearly directly." The second level, the cortical primary projection areas, "represent all parts of the body doubly indirectly." The highest level, the so-called association areas, "are evolved out of the middle as the middle are evolved out of the lowest and the lowest are out of the periphery." These association areas of the highest level, beyond perception, are concerned with concepts and cognition. For Jackson they were "the organ of the mind."

177. Edelman 2004, 156.

178. Crick 1994, 234.

179. Koch 2004, 336.

180. Hobson 1999, 72.

181. Pope 1733, Epistle II, An Essay on Man.

Chapter 4 Where It Begins: Anatomy and Environment

1. This notion of three concentric layers of nervous system, each representing a respective layer of three concentric environments, was introduced to me by Paul Yakovlev, who I believe first formulated it. So far as I know, it was never published by him.

2. Excision of the affective component of experience can occur in isolation without altering the perceptual parallel. Years ago, I was asked to see a patient who had recovered from a stroke. On clinical grounds, for this was before the days of computer imaging, he had suffered a "top of the basilar" infarct affecting medial temporal lobe. He came to me because "he didn't understand things." When asked what he did not understand he reported that it was mainly things he read. I gave him a full-page four-color advertisement in a glossy magazine to read silently. The ad depicted a curvaceous Hollywood starlet who said (I paraphrase) that her livelihood depended on her good looks, her good looks depended on getting a good night's sleep, and a good night's sleep depended on having a mattress that adapted to her curves. She then recommended the mattress being advertised.

When he finished reading I took back the magazine and asked the patient to tell me about it. "

Well," he said, "It's an ad." (The quotes are reconstructions.)

I thought that a good starting summary. "What are they selling?" I asked.

"Mattresses," he said.

"Tell me about it," I requested.

"Well," he said, "A pretty Hollywood actress needs a good night's sleep to keep her good looks so she uses the mattress they are selling."

"That's it," I said. "That's correct."

"Yeah," he said. "But I'll tell you something. I didn't understand it."

I don't believe he was trying to mislead me. I simply did not have the tools to measure what he was describing.

Chapter 5 Where It Began: Evolution

1. Cobb, in Locke 1969, 2.
2. Glynn 1999, 164.
3. Noback and Moscowitz, in Beuttner-Janusch 1962, 210.
4. Herrick 1948, 162.
5. Clark 1960, 228.
6. Webster II: 1934, 838.

Chapter 6 What Is It?: Consciousness

1. Libet 1999, 13.
2. Libet 1999, 56.
3. Schacter, in Gazzaniga 2000, 1274.

Chapter 8 See Here: Attention

1. Kryger et al. 1989, 1026.
2. Steriade, in Kryger et al. 1989, 112.
3. Posner and Digirolamo, in Gazzaniga 2000, 623.
4. Posner and Digirolamo, in Gazzaniga 2000, 625.
5. Posner and Digirolamo, in Gazzaniga 2000, 626.
6. *Ibid*.
7. Mangun et al., in Gazzaniga 2000, 702.
8. Dehaene et al. 2006, *Cognitive Sciences* 10, 204–211.
9. Mangun et al., in Gazzaniga 2000, 705.

10. Chelazzi and Corbetta, in Gazzaniga 2000, 667.
11. Steriade, in Kryger et al. 1989, 112.

Chapter 9 Perchance to Dream: Sleep

1. Searle *NYRB* 53, 51.
2. Carskadon and Dement, in Kryger et al. 1989, 16.

Chapter 10 $x = 2y$: Representation

1. Merikle and Daneman, in Gazzaniga 2000, 1297.
2. Bellass et al. 1988, *Neuropsychologia* 26, 45–52.
3. Laberge, in Gazzaniga 2000, 715.
4. An ironic aside is that we pride ourselves on being the most intelligent animal and demand that less intelligent creatures, such as chimpanzees, learn our language instead of using our intelligence to learn their language.

Chapter 11 The Dance of Life: Movement

1. "If they ask you 'what is the sign of your Father in you?' Say to them 'movement and rest.'" Gospel of St. Thomas 50 NHL 125. Quoted in Pagels, E. Beyond Belief: The Secret Gospel of Thomas. Random House, NY 2003.
2. Humphrey 2006, 104.
3. Choudhury and Blakemore, in Pockett et al. 2006, 49.

Chapter 12 They All Fall Down: Dissolution of Function

1. In America, during the first half of the twentieth century, two trends of investigation in the behavioral sciences developed simultaneously. One, exemplified by Skinner and his followers, consisted of introducing a variable into the artificially structured laboratory environment and recording the response of the resident animal. The second, largely championed by the ethologists at the American Museum of Natural History, consisted of going into the field and watching.

It has always seemed to me that the second method is the more sensitive even in the examination of the neurologically injured human. The patient who can raise both arms promptly and correctly in response to command may, during presentation of the medical history, gesture exclusively with the left hand. If the examiner does not ask, "Why is this right-handed patient not using his right hand for emphasis?" he or she will miss the presence of a deficit. The minimal stimuli of real life can be overridden by the imposed stronger stimuli of the formal structured situation. And it takes minimal stimuli to display minor response deficits.

Often dynamic imaging studies employ tasks designed for the investigative situation. The outcome of the study gives good information relative to the study— this is the way blood flows in this study—but may give only incomplete information about daily life encounters. The mental task required during the PET or MRI scan is biologically less significant than the stimuli of daily life and may tell little about brain responses to stimuli located elsewhere on the stimulus hierarchy. In addition, the role of context in this kind of (really in all) testing is ignored.
2. Passingham and Lau, in Pockett 2006, 67.

3. Owen et al. 2006, 1402.
4. Kinsbourne 2006, 873.

Chapter 14 Which Have Eyes and See Not: Stimulus Hierarchy

1. The correct question to ask is, "*If* I were to ask you, 'Which is the road to Tucson?' what would you tell me?" Alternative solutions also require the "if" component, explicit or implied.

2. The problem is that Anton's original description included a potpourri of causes.

Chapter 16 Play It Again: Speculative Reprise

1. An analogy for conscious awareness can be constructed, though it is a conceptual model and not to be construed as a statement of how the physiologic process actually works; but it is conceivable that the physiologic process *could* work this way.

The electron beam (Z-axis) of a standard oscilloscope is set so low that it hardly activates the phosphorescent screen. As usual, the X- and Y-axes display time and event, respectively. The Y-axis is set so that, above a low-level voltage, the information is fed back to the Z-axis, increasing its electron output. This brightens the beam and displays the event sharply against the low level of the trace below the critical voltage.

In this analogy the low-level Z-beam corresponds to the consciousness generated by the ascending reticular activating system to cause readiness. The phosphorescent screen is analogous to the cortex. The feedback is the perceptual event, and the brightening of the electron beam is the change in consciousness to produce awareness, or focusing of attention.

The positive feedback, or recursion, from the specific perceptual system to the nonspecific consciousness system does not imply the need for separate modules. The same module, perhaps arranged in different assemblies, with or without additions or deletions, could generate both functions.

The analog of the subliminal experience—unconscious perception or perception without awareness—would occur when the voltage of the displayed event did not reach the critical level required to produce feedback. On the oscilloscope, the event is displayed but not brightened.

2. The importance of lesions that produce lateralized inattention or loss of consciousness in a field of awareness is to allow demonstration in isolation of each member of the consciousness–perception duo. Perception is retained, as can be demonstrated with single stimuli (several modalities) in the affected field. Consciousness is suppressed, as can be demonstrated with double simultaneous stimulation, but it can be restored by increasing the spatial or temporal characteristics of the neglected stimulus.

This raises three interesting questions that have only speculative answers: 1) Following injury, how is the percept made conscious? 2) Why is that consciousness suppressed when competing stimuli are offered? 3) What permits recovery of the consciousness with spatial or temporal summation?

A possible formulation is based on the interchangeability of the consciousness-producing modules which lack modality markers. When a given assembly is injured in one hemisphere (usually the right), the homologous assembly in the other hemisphere provides support by way of commissural fibers (transcallosal connections of homologous cortical areas are well demonstrated, so this, at least, is not speculation) when the stimuli are limited to the fields of the affected hemisphere. When competitive stimuli appear in the contralateral field, the transcallosal support is withdrawn in favor of the exigent needs of the competing stimulus—exigent because it is in the contralateral field, a lower level, and therefore in a more demanding relationship. Only by increasing the amount of the suppressed stimulus can overflow sufficient for commissural transfer once again occur.

3. Kinsbourne 2006, 873.
4. Pockett 2006, 11.
5. Freeman, in Pockett 2006, 76.
6. Pacherie, in Pockett 2006, 146.
7. Pacherie, in Pockett 2006, 147.
8. Mele, in Pockett 2006, 191.
9. Pacherie, in Pockett 2006, 151.
10. Malle, in Pockett 2006, 226.
11. It has been said that it is better to be interesting than to be right.

Readings on Consciousness

Books

Blackburn, S. *Think: A Compelling Introduction to Philosophy*. Oxford: Oxford University Press, 1999.

Chalmers, D. J. *The Conscious Mind*. New York: Oxford University Press, 1996.

Crick, F. *The Astonishing Hypothesis: The Scientific Search for the Soul*. New York: Touchstone, Simon and Schuster, 1994.

Dennett, D. C. *Kinds of Minds: Toward an Understanding of Consciousness*. New York: Basic Books, 1996.

Edelman, G. M. *Wider Than the Sky: The Phenomenal Gift of Consciousness*. New Haven, CT: Yale University Press, 2004.

Gazzaniga, M. S. *The New Cognitive Neurosciences*, 2nd edition. Cambridge, MA: MIT Press, 2000.

Hobson, J. A. *Consciousness*. New York, Scientific American Library, 1999.

Honderich, T. *On Consciousness*. Pittsburgh, PA: University of Pittsburgh Press, 2004.

Humphrey, N. *Seeing Red: A Study in Consciousness*. Cambridge, MA: Belknap Press, 2006.

Koch, C. *The Quest for Consciousness: A Neurobiological Approach*. Englewood, CO: Roberts and Company, 2004.

Libet, B. *Mind Time: The Temporal Factor in Consciousness*. Cambridge, MA: Harvard University Press, 2004.

McKeon, R., ed. *The Basic Works of Aristotle: De Anima, Book II, Chapter 5.* New York: Random House, 1941.

Metzinger, T., ed. *Neural Correlates of Consciousness.* Cambridge, MA: MIT Press, 2000.

Pockett, S., W. P. Banks, and S. Gallagher. *Does Consciousness Cause Behavior?* Cambridge, MA: MIT Press, 2006.

Searle, J. R. *Mind: A Brief Introduction.* Oxford: Oxford University Press, 2004.

Articles

Chalmers, D. J. 1997. "Consciousness and the philosophers: an exchange." *New York Review of Books* 44:8.

Dehaene, S., J. P. Changeux, J. S. Naccache, and C. Sergent. 2006. "Conscious, preconscious and subliminal processing: a testable taxonomy." *Trends in Cognitive Sciences* 10:204–211.Harnad, S. 2005. "What is consciousness?" *New York Review of Books* 52:11.

Kinsbourne, M. 2006. "From unilateral neglect to the brain basis of consciousness." *Cortex* 42:869–874.

Libet, B. 1999. "How does conscious experience arise?" *Brain Research Bulletin* 50:339–340.

Naccache, L. 2006. "Is she conscious?" *Science* 313:1395–1396.

Owen, A. M., M. R. Coleman, M. Boly, M. H. Davis, S. Laureys, and J. D. Pickard. 2006. "Detecting awareness in the vegetative state." *Science* 313:1402.

Rosenthal, D. M. 2002. "The timing of conscious states." *Consciousness and Cognition* 11:215–220.

Searle, J. R. 1995. "The mystery of consciousness." *New York Review of Books* 42 (17)(18).

Searle, J. R. 2005. "Consciousness: what we still don't know." *New York Review of Books* 52 (1):36–39 .

Searle, J. R. 2006. "Minding the brain." *New York Review of Books* 53 (17):51–55.

Zeman, A. 2001. "Consciousness." *Brain* 124:1263–1289.

Related Readings

Books

Adrian, E.D. *The Mechanism of Nervous Action*. Philadelphia, PA: University of Pennsylvania Press, 1932.

Bailey, G.V., and P. Bonin. *Isocortex of Man*. Urbana, IL: University of Illinois Press, 1951.

Bargman, W., and J.T. Schade, eds. *Rhinencephalon and Related Structures*. Amsterdam: Elsevier, 1963.

Bass, A.D., *Evolution of Nervous Control from Primitive Organism to Man*. Washington, D.C.: AAAS, 1959.

Beech, F.A., D.O. Hebb, C.V Morgan, and H.W. Nissan, eds. *The Neuropsychology of Lashley: Selected Papers of K. S. Lashley*. New York: McGraw Hill, 1960.

Benton, A.L. *Right-Left Discrimination and Finger Location*. New York: Hoeber-Harper, 1959.

Beutner-Janusch, J., ed. *The Relatives of Man: Modern Studies of the Relation of the Evolution of Nonhuman Primates to Human Evolution*. New York: Annals of the New York Academy of Sciences, 1962.

Brodal, A. *Reticular Formation of the Brainstem*. Edinborough, UK: Oliver and Boyd, 1957.

Clark, W. E. LeGros. *The Antecedents of Man*. Chicago: Quadrangle Books, 1960.

Coghill, G.E. *Anatomy and the Problem of Behavior*. New York: Hafner, 1929, rpr. 1964.

Creed, R.S., D.E. Denny-Brown, J.C. Eccles, E.G.T. Liddell, and C.S. Sherrington. *Reflex Activity of the Spinal Cord*. Oxford: Clarendon Press, 1932.

Delisle Burns, D. *The Mammalian Cerebral Cortex*. London: Arnold, 1958.

Denny-Brown, D.E. *Selected Writings of Sir Charles Sherrington*. New York: Paul B. Hoeber, 1940.

Denny-Brown, D.E. *The Cerebral Control of Movement*. Liverpool, UK: Liverpool University Press, 1966.

Eccles, J.C. *Neurophysiologic Basis of Mind*. Oxford: Clarendon Press, 1953.

Eccles, J.C. *The Understanding of the Brain*. New York: McGraw Hill, 1973.

Economo, C.V. *L' Architecture Cellulare Normale de l'Ecorce Cerebrale*. Paris: Masson, 1927.

Edelman, G.M., and V.B. Mountcastle. *The Mindful Brain*. Cambridge, MA: MIT Press, 1978.

Fentress, J.C., ed. *Simpler Networks and Behavior*. Sunderland, MA: Sinauer, 1976.

Fulton, J.F., and A.D. Kellar. The *Sign of Babinski: The Study of the Evolution of Cortical Dominance in Primates*. Springfield, IL: C. C. Thomas, 1932.

Gastaut, H., and H.J. Lammers. *Anatomie du Rhinencephale*. Paris: Masson, 1961.

Geschwind, N. *Disconnection Syndromes in Animal and Man*. London: St. Martin's Press, 1965.

Glynn, I. *An Anatomy of Thought*. Oxford: Oxford University Press, 1999.

Goldstein, K. *The Organism*. New York: American Book Company, 1939.

Goldstein, K. *Human Nature*. Cambridge, MA: Harvard University Press, 1951.

Granit, R. *Receptors and Sensory Perception*. New Haven, CT: Yale University Press, 1956.

Gregory, R.L., ed. *The Oxford Companion to the Mind*. Oxford: Oxford University Press, 1987.

Haecan, J., and J.D. Ajuriaguerra. *Left Handedness*. New York: Grune and Stratton, 1964.

Harman, P.J. *Paleoneurologic, Neoneurologic and Ontogenetic Aspects of Brain Phylogeny*. New York: American Museum of Natural History, 1957.

Head, H. *Studies in Neurology: Henry Frowde*, 2 vols. London: Oxford University Press, 1920.

Head, H. *Aphasia*, 2 vols. New York: Hafner, 1963.

Hebb, D.O.: The Organization of Behavior.: New York: Wiley. New York, 1949.

Herrick, C.J. *Brains of Rats and Men*. Chicago: University of Chicago Press, 1926.

Herrick, C.J. *The Brain of the Tiger Salamander*. Chicago: University of Chicago Press, 1948.

Herrick, C.J. *Evolution of Human Nature*. Austin, TX: University of Texas Press, 1956.

Herrick, C.J. *Neurological Foundations of Animal Behavior*. New York: Hafner, 1962.

Hooker, D. *Prenatal Origin of Behavior*. Lawrence: University of Kansas Press, 1952.

Hooker, D. *Evidence of Prenatal Function of the Nervous System*. New York: American Museum of Natural History, 1958.

Ivanov-Smolensky, A.G. *Essays on the Pathophysiology of the Higher Nervous Activity*. Moscow: Foreign Languages Publishing House, 1954.

Kauffman, S. *At Home in the Universe*. Oxford: Oxford University Press, 1995.

Kryger, M.H., T. Roth, and W.C. Dement. *Principles and Practice of Sleep Medicine*. Philadelphia: W. B. Saunders, 1989.

Kuffler, S.W., and J.G. Nicholls. From *Neuron to Brain*. Sunderland, MA: Sinauer, 1976.

Locke, S. ed. *Modern Neurology*. Boston: Little Brown, 1969.

Lowenstein, W.R. ed. *Principles of Receptor Physiology*. New York: Springer, 1971.

Luria, A.R. *Higher Cortical Functions in Man*. New York: Basic Books, 1966.

Luria, A.R. *Human Brain and Psychological Processes*. New York: Harper and Row, 1966.

Magoun, H.W., and R. Rhines. *Spasticity: The Stretch Reflex and Extrapyramidal Systems*. Springfield, IL: C. C. Thomas, 1947.

Magoun, H.W. *The Waking Brain*. Springfield, IL: C. C. Thomas, 1948.

Maier, N.R.F., and T.C. Schneirla. *Principles of Animal Psychology*. New York: McGraw Hill, 1935.

Mettler, F.A. *Culture and the Structural Evolution of the Nervous System*. New York: American Museum of Natural History, 1956.

Morgan, E. *The Descent of the Child: Human Evolution From a New Perspective*. New York: Oxford University Press, 1995.

Mostofsky, D.E. ed. *Attention: Contemporary Theory and Analysis*. New York: Appleton Century Crofts, 1970.

Mountcastle, V.B., ed. *Interhemispheric Relations and Cerebral Dominance*. Baltimore: Johns Hopkins University Press, 1962.

Nielsen, J.M. *Agnosia, Apraxia, Aphasia*. New York: Hafner, 1948, rpr. 1962.

Papez, J.W. *Comparative Neurology*. New York: Hafner, nd.

Penfield, W.G. *Excitable Cortex in Conscious Man*. Springfield, IL: C. C. Thomas, 1967.

Penfield, W. G., and T.C. Erickson. *Epilepsy and Cerebral Localization*. Springfield, IL: C. C. Thomas, 1941.

Piaget, J. *Structuralism*. New York: Harper Colophon Books, 1970.

Purpura, D.P., and G.P. Reaser. *Methodological Approaches to the Study of Brain Maturation and its Abnormalities*. Baltimore, MD: University Park Press, 1974.

Rasmussen, G.L., and W.F. Windle, ed. *Neural Mechanisms of the Auditory and Vestibular Systems*. Springfield, IL: C. C. Thomas, 1960.

Refsum, S., et al: *The So-Called Extrapyramidal System*. Oslo: Universitets Forlagets, 1963.

Schimmel, S. *The Seven Deadly Sins*. New York: The Free Press, 1992.

Semmes, J., S.Weinstein, L. Ghent, and H.L. Teuber. *Somatosensory Changes After Penetrating Brain Wounds in Man*. Cambridge, MA: Harvard University Press, 1960.

Shagass, C., S. Gershon, and A.J. Friedhoff. *Psychopathology and Brain Dysfunction*. New York: Raven Press, 1977.

Sheer, D.E., ed. *Electrical Stimulation of the Brain*. Austin: University of Texas Press, 1961.

Sherrington, C.S. *The Brain and Its Mechanisms (Rede Lecture)*. Cambridge, UK: Cambridge University Press, 1933.

Sherrington, C.S. *Integrative Action of the Nervous System*. Cambridge, UK: Cambridge University Press, 1947.

Taylor, J. *Selected Writings of John Hughlings Jackson*, 2 vols. New York: Basic Books, 1958.

Teuber, H.L., W.S. Battersby, and M. Bender. *Visual Field Defects After Penetrating Wounds of the Brain*. Cambridge, MA: Harvard University Press, 1960.

Tulving, E., and W. Donaldson, eds. *Organization of Memory*. New York: Academic Press, 1972.

Vaina, L., ed. *From the Retina to the Neocortex—Selected Papers of David Marr*. Boston, MA: Birkhauser, 1991.

Valverde, F. *Studies on the Piriform Lobe*. Cambridge, MA: Harvard University Press, 1965.

Walshe, F.M.R. *Critical Studies in Neurology*. Edinborough, UK: Livingston, 1948.

Willis, T. *The Anatomy of the Brain*. Tuckahoe, NY: U.S.V. Pharmaceutical Corporation, 1971.

Young, F. and D. Lindsley. *Early Experience and Visual Information Processing*. Washington, D.C.: National Academy of Sciences, 1970.

Zangwill, O.L. *Cerebral Dominance and its Relation to Psychological Function*. Edinborough, UK: Oliver and Boyd, 1960.

Articles

Anton, G. 1899. "Über die selbstwahrnehmung der herderkrankungen des gehirns durch den kranken bei rindenblindheit und rindentaubheit." *Archiv für Psychiatrie und Nervenkrankheiten, Berlin* 32:86–127.

Bellas, S. D., R. A. Novelly, B. Eskenazi, and J. Wasserstein. 1988. "The nature of unilateral neglect in the olfactory sensory system." *Neuropsychologia* 26:45–52.

Broadbent, D. E. 1964. "Vigilance." *British Medical Bulletin* 20:17–20.

Deeke, L., P. Scheid, and H.H. Kornhuber. 1969. "Distribution of readiness potential, pre-motion positivity and motor potential of the human cerebral cortex preceding voluntary finger movements." *Experimental Brain Research* 7:158–168.

Denny-Brown, D. E., J. S. Meyer, and S. Horenstein. 1952. "The significance of perceptual rivalry resulting from parietal lobe lesions." *Brain* 75:433–471.

Effron, R. 1970. "The relationship between the duration of stimulus and the duration of a perception." *Neuropsychologia* 8:37–55.

Evarts, E. V. 1973. "Brain mechanisms in movement." *Scientific American* 229:96–103.

Geschwind, N. 1972. "Cerebral dominance and anatomic asymmetry." *NE Journal of Medicine* 287:194–195.

Gross, C. G., D. B. Bender, and C. E. Rocha-Miranda. 1969. "Visual receptive fields of neurons in the inferotemporal cortex of the monkey." *Science* 166:1303–1305.

Lawrence, D. G., and H. G. Kuypers. 1968a. "The functional organization of the motor system in the monkey: I. The effects of bilateral pyramidal lesions." *Brain* 91:1–14.

Lawrence, D. G., and H. G. Kuypers. 1968b. "The functional organization of the motor system in the monkey. II. The effects of lesions of the descending brain-stem pathways." *Brain* 91:15–36.

Lezine, I. 1973. "The transition from sensorimotor to earliest symbolic function in early development." *Research Publication of the Association for Research in Nervous and Mental Diseases* 51:221–232.

Lindsley, D. B., J. W. Bowden, and H. W. Magoun. 1949. "Effect upon the EEG of acute injury to the brainstem activating system." *Electroencephalography and Clinical Neurophysiology* 1:475–486.

Livingstone, M. S., and D. H. Hubel. 1981. "Effects of sleep and arousal on the processing of visual information in the cat." *Nature* 291:554–561.

Locke, S., and L. Kellar. 1973. "Categorical perception in a nonlinguistic mode." *Cortex* 9:355–369.

Meltzoff, A. N., and M. K. Moore. 1977. "Imitation of facial and manual gestures by human neonates." *Science* 198:75–78.

Morruzzi, G., and H. W. Magoun. 1949. "Brainstem reticular formation and activation of the EEG." *Electroencephalography and Clinical Neurophysiology* 1:455–473.

Munk, M. H. J., P. R. Roelfsema, P. Konig, A. K. Engel, and W. Singer. 1996. "Role of reticular activation in the modulation of intracortical synchronization." *Science* 272:271–274.

Riddoch, G. 1917. "Dissociation of visual perception due to occipital injuries, with special reference to the appreciation of movement." *Brain* 40:15–57.

Rizzolatti, G., and L. Craighero. 2004. "The Mirror-Neuron System." *Annual Review of Neuroscience* 27: 169-192

Rosadini, G., and G. F. Rossi. 1967. "On the suggested cerebral dominance for consciousness." *Brain* 90:101–112.

Schapiro, S., and K. R. Vukovich. 1970. "Early experience effects on cortical dendrites." *Science* 167:292–294.

Serafetinides, E. A., R. D. Hoare, and M. Drive. 1965. "Intracarotid sodium amylobarbitone and cerebral dominance for speech and consciousness." *Brain* 88:107–130.

Sergeev, G. A., and L. A. Panashchenko. 1970. "On the influence of digital training on the functional state of the cerebral cortex in children in their first postnatal year according to EEG data." *Zhurnal Vysshei Nervnoi Deyatel'nosti* 20:1290–1291.

Tyler, H. R. 1969. "Defective stimulus exploration in aphasic patients." *Neurology* 19:105–112.

Yingling, C. 1975. "Motor programs and feedback in control of movement." *BIS Conference Report* 38:65–73.

Index

About the Author

SIMEON LOCKE spent fifty years on the neurology faculty of Harvard Medical School. Among the many roles he has taken during his career, he has been acting chief of neurology at Boston City Hospital, chief of neurology at Boston State Hospital, and chief of neurology at New England Deaconess Hospital (now Beth Israel Deaconess Medical Center).